PRAISE FOR EMPOWERED BOUNDARIES

"Storm outlines—quite comprehensively—what it means to have a dynamic self in relationship to others that is both honoring of ourselves and conscious of our coexistence with others. *Empowered Boundaries* is practical and soulful and an impressive contribution to many different lineages of thought—psychology, social movements, and social justice education."

—LIZ GOODWIN, coauthor with Leticia Nieto
of *Beyond Inclusion, Beyond Empowerment: A
Developmental Strategy to Liberate Everyone*

"With a history steeped in self-defense, decades' worth of de-escalation skills, and a lifelong interest in the nefarious workings of white nationalists, Cristien Storm is the absolute perfect person to write this timely and important book."

—INGA MUSCIO, author of *Cunt: A Declaration
of Independence, Autobiography of a Blue-Eyed
Devil: My Life and Times in a Racist Imperialist
Society,* and *Rose: Love in Violent Times*

"Cristien Storm's *Empowered Boundaries* couldn't come at a better time. In an era of bully culture, when decisions often get made by those who don't hesitate to take what they want, while the rest of us keep worrying whether pushing back might make it worse, Storm shows us how to say, 'Enough!' We are lucky to have such a ferocious fighter and such a loving listener in our midst and even luckier that she has shared her hard-won wisdom to help us train our minds, our hearts, and our fists to claim the space for lives worth living."

—SHON MECKFESSEL, author of *Nonviolence
Ain't What It Used to Be: Unarmed Insurrection
and the Rhetoric of Resistance*

"This hands-on guide to setting and upholding strong boundaries belongs on everyone's bookshelf. It brings together Cristien Storm's experience teaching women's self-defense, organizing against white nationalism, creating art, and supporting people in their personal healing to create an eminently readable resource to developing the skills and tools we need to be happy, whole, and safe. This is an inviting, practical, and essential book."

—DAN BERGER, associate professor of comparative ethnic studies at the University of Washington at Bothell, coauthor with Toussaint Losier of *Rethinking the American Prison Movement*, and author of *The Struggle Within: Prisons, Political Prisoners,* and *Mass Movements in the United States*

EMPOWERED BOUNDARIES

EMPOWERED
BOUNDARIES

SPEAKING TRUTH, SETTING BOUNDARIES, AND INSPIRING SOCIAL CHANGE

CRISTIEN STORM

North Atlantic Books
Berkeley, California

Published by　　　　　　　　　　　Cover design by Jasmine Hromjak
North Atlantic Books　　　　　　　Book design by Happenstance Type-O-Rama
Berkeley, California 94712

Printed in the United States of America

Empowered Boundaries: Speaking Truth, Setting Boundaries, and Inspiring Social Change is sponsored and published by the Society for the Study of Native Arts and Sciences (dba North Atlantic Books), an educational nonprofit based in Berkeley, California, that collaborates with partners to develop cross-cultural perspectives, nurture holistic views of art, science, the humanities, and healing, and seed personal and global transformation by publishing work on the relationship of body, spirit, and nature.

North Atlantic Books' publications are available through most bookstores. For further information, visit our website at www.northatlanticbooks.com or call 800-733-3000.

Library of Congress Cataloguing-in-Publication data is
available from the publisher upon request.

1 2 3 4 5 6 7 8 9 KPC 22 21 20 19 18

Printed on recycled paper

North Atlantic Books is committed to the protection of our environment. We partner with FSC-certified printers using soy-based inks and print on recycled paper whenever possible.

CONTENTS

////////////////////////////

ACKNOWLEDGMENTS. IX

PROLOGUE. XI

INTRODUCTION 1

— PART I —

ONE: WHAT IS A BOUNDARY?. 13

TWO: LEARNING TO SET BOUNDARIES 23

THREE: CHALLENGES AND DOUBTS. 41

FOUR: INTUITION AND THE REFLECTIVE LOOP 53

FIVE: GOALS AND CHALLENGES IN SETTING, DEFENDING, OR
NEGOTIATING BOUNDARIES 67

SIX: COMPASSION AND BOUNDARIES. 85

— PART II —

SEVEN: SAFETY IN A CULTURE OF FEAR 97

EIGHT: SETTING BOUNDARIES WITH INTENTION 113

NINE: CREATING AND UNDERSTANDING SUPPORTS FOR
BOUNDARY SETTING. 127

TEN: LEARNING SELF-CARE AND SELF-ACCEPTANCE. 139

ELEVEN: COMMUNITY CARE AND SOCIAL CHANGE 153

TWELVE: WRAPPING IT ALL UP 165

EXERCISES. 169

ABOUT THE AUTHOR. 183

ACKNOWLEDGMENTS

IT IS WITH THE LOVE, SUPPORT, AND COMMITMENT OF SO MANY PEOPLE that projects such as this are brought into the world. I would like to thank some of those people here. I want to thank Alison Knowles for reaching out and believing in this book and Ebonie Ledbetter and Julia Sadowski, as well as everyone at North Atlantic Books for making *Empowered Boundaries* happen. Barbara Sjoholm, thanks so much for your support, insight, suggestions, and editing. Deborah May Wilk, thank you for walking with me on my most challenging journeys; you are one fantastic mentor. Steve Payne, thank you for being a solid support beam in the early days of Home Alive.

Home Alive founders Julie Hasse, Gretta Harley, Stacey Wescott, Valerie Agnew, Zoe Bermet, Lara Kidoguchi, Jessica Lawless, and Mich Levy—you all helped create an organization, a mindset, and nurtured the seeds for this book. Thank you also to each and every Home Alive staff member, volunteer, collective member, instructor, board member, and supporter—thank you for showing up and doing the work. Ajax, thank you for always being there. Thank you to all the people who have supported me over the years in so many ways. I am grateful to those of you who have challenged me, loved me, pushed me, hugged me, performed with me, and taught me things I may or may not have wanted to know. Thank you to all the trainers, organizers, activists, writers, dreamers, and each and every one of you who work to make this world a better place.

PROLOGUE
/////////////////////////

As this book comes to print, mainstream America is being introduced to white nationalism, a dangerous social movement whose genocidal vision is the creation of a white homeland through the removal of all people of color, all Jewish people, and any dissenters. Its attempted ascension is focused on occupying the State in order to build a white ethnic nation state.[1] Mainstream America is also grappling with understanding the difference between white supremacy and the social movement of white nationalism. As Eric K. Ward, a social justice educator, puts it, "White nationalism is always white supremacist but white supremacy is not always white nationalist."[2]

What does this have to do with boundaries?

Our boundaries are political whether we want them to be or not. Our boundaries, whether they are set via action or inaction, whether they are proactive or reactive, establish the culture and sensibilities of our relationships and the spaces we move through. When we do not respond to a sexist comment, for example, the space becomes one in which sexism can expand, which in turn creates conditions where escalating sexist behaviors are more possible. However, if

---

[1] If You Don't They Will: A Pocket Guide to Fighting White Nationalism, www.racefiles.com /2017/10/03/put-some-knowledge-in-your-pocket/.

[2] Erik K. Ward, "As White Supremacy Falls Down, White Nationalism Stands Up," Pop Collab, October 31, 2017, http://popcollab.org/white-supremacy-falls-white-nationalism-stands/.

we can assert a clear boundary in the face of a sexist comment, we demark that space as one where sexism is not tolerated. Boundaries then, are not just individual and interpersonal but social as well. What this means is that boundaries are important, not only for how we move through the world as individuals but also for how we create, nurture, respond to, and shape the spaces we inhabit. Therefore, our boundaries are not just about responding to individual interactions, but also about envisioning and creating the kinds of communities we want to live in. This may involve responding to a discriminatory comment, agitating for systemic change in a work environment, promoting underrepresented leadership, building solidarity between grassroots organizing projects, supporting local community-based groups, becoming active in neighborhood actions, and/or joining political movements for social justice. This is not in any way an attempt to blame those who are experiencing oppressions for not responding "the right way" or an attempt to blame the cause of sexism on a lack of "good" boundaries. Let me be clear: sexism, like racism, homophobia, and gender bias, is systemic and rooted in both white nationalism and white supremacy. In addition, I do not want to imply that everyone has to respond to every hateful or oppressive comment or behavior. We must all pick and choose our battles, which are informed by our resources, abilities, accessibilities, safety, family history, support networks, and a million other aspects that contribute to who and how we are in the world.

I grew into young adulthood going to punk rock shows in the Bay Area. The music and the music scene helped me deal with the trauma I was trying to survive and gave a subcultural sanction to express the rage and pain I felt. The music spaces also allowed me to use and move my body in ways that felt empowering. An embodied sense of empowerment is important for everybody to feel, but is especially true for survivors of trauma since trauma overwhelms the body and can make one feel small, helpless, and ineffective. I also learned important lessons about boundaries. Nazi punks, racist skinheads, white power bands, and people who would later be identified as white nationalists were all not allowed in our music community. While racism, sexism, and homophobia are of course present in every scene, I learned the importance of setting different kinds of boundaries early on. The kinds of boundaries we used when someone in our community said something oppressive out of ignorance were very different than the boundaries we used when someone was clearly advocating a position based in heteronormative white supremacy or white nationalism. Being hurt and defensive is common when people are called out (or in) for oppressive language and behaviors. Defensiveness, however, is very different from promoting white supremacist values and beliefs; it entails being unwilling to change one's viewpoint and actually trying to change other people's values and beliefs to the hateful ones being espoused. It is important to remember that white nationalism is a social movement that seeks to create a white ethnic nation state; this means white nationalists are organizing for their version of "social change," just as those of us fighting for collective liberation are organizing. It is not always easy to distinguish someone attempting to organize in a space from someone repeating oppressive rhetoric yet also open to change when confronted. It is important, however, to find ways to differentiate these positions because they require different kinds of boundaries. Setting these very different kinds of boundaries was often a messy and complicated process. But it became clear to me how critical it was to be able to navigate and set these types of boundaries in order to create the kinds of spaces we wanted. If someone was trying to organize in our community by promoting white supremacy, no matter what the language ("We just want our own safe space too, it's just a different opinion. It's not hateful to be proud of being white" or, "Reverse racism is real and hurts white people ..."), the boundary needed to clearly and in no uncertain terms identify our space as anti-racist. If someone was open to conversation and committed to nurturing and supporting vibrant anti-racist spaces, they were welcome. Our music community was, of course, imperfect, but theses kinds of boundaries were important attempts at building the kinds of relationships and communities we dared to envision and fight for. In this current moment of rising white nationalism and emboldened white supremacy, we need these kinds of boundaries more than ever.

When racist skinheads or those espousing white supremacy or nazi ideology claimed they had a right to be at a show, or that kicking them out was censorship or intolerance, our response was a clear and resounding "No. You don't have a right to be here." Further, we asserted, "You have a right to your ideology but you do not have the right to spew it here. Not in my house, not in my show, not in my classroom, not in my bar, not in my book club. Because if you are here asserting the inhumanity of certain people, the space is no longer accessible or safe for them and that is unacceptable." This lesson in boundaries showed me the power of saying no so that I could also say yes. We kicked hardcore nazis out so that we could have generative discussions about how to address racism, sexism, and homophobia in our spaces without having to constantly defend the need to do that work. This was not always easy. Learning how to grapple with these issues and set boundaries around them was challenging to be sure, but absolutely necessary. We must contend with the complexities of this kind of boundary work in order to move toward collective liberation.[3]

One thing I learned through my experiences of kicking organized nazis out of our music communities was how often asserting something in the form of "my opinion" could effectively shut down opposition to whatever was being espoused. My friends and I struggled with how to respond to claims of free speech and a right to state one's opinion. It was assumed that every opinion held the same weight (as if some opinions are not more legitimized through historical legacies of privilege and power), and that everyone was equally entitled to his or her opinion (as if the social, political, and economic playing field was level—it is not). While it is true that everyone is entitled to their opinion, it is also true that people do not have the right to share it in any space at any time. You will not be allowed to spew racist rhetoric in my house, for

---

[3] For more on countering white nationalism, please check out "If You Don't They Will: A Pocket Guide to Fighting White Nationalism."

example. All the collectives and nonprofits I've worked with had clear mission and values statements demarking what language and behaviors were permissible. Clubs and bars often have signs about what behaviors and language will get someone kicked out, and businesses of all kinds have codes of conduct. Using this logic, we learned to cut clear boundaries in our spaces—just because you have a right to your opinion does not mean you get to share it when you want to and however you want to. In addition, there are things that are not opinions, such as the idea that white people are superior to people of color, that trans people deserve to die, that Jewish people control the media, or that women are inferior to men. When these violent beliefs are transmuted into "just a different opinion" it is an attempt to flatten power differences, ignore historical realities and inequities, create false moral equivalencies, and advocate for oppression and subjugation under the guise of "opinion." Fascism, like white nationalism, white supremacy, and heteropatriarchy, is not just an opinion; it is a dangerous and violent ideology that must be countered. Boundaries are essential to this work.

I brought my punk rock roots and the sensibility of both *no* and *yes* into adulthood and the work I did with nonprofits and collective organizations. For example, in response to an allegation of sexual assault, when someone would say there are two sides to every story and they needed to be listened to as well, the *no* and *yes* framework that had developed through countering white supremacy and white nationalism became useful. It is true that there are multiple perspectives to all events and it is important to listen to people. Listening is essential to boundary setting. There is a difference, however, between someone who will never acknowledge (or does not believe in) the complexities of consent and the role that intergenerational, gender-based trauma and sexism play in shaping how women and female-identified folks respond in certain situations, and someone who is open to understanding why and how sexism and gender violence operate and shape experiences. If someone is not open to the possibility of shifting their beliefs (or clearly against addressing sexism and gender-based violence, like in this example), then our boundaries must be different.

As we face the alarming rise of white nationalism and emboldened white supremacy, it seems imperative to me that our boundary work include an understanding of how to say "No. Not ever" to white nationalism and fascist tendencies while saying, "Yes" to all kinds of solidarity work. Both kinds of boundaries are necessary in organizing for collective liberation. The personal is political, the political is personal, and our boundaries must embody our individual wants and needs as well as our political and social sensibilities. I hope you find creative and inspired ways to weave these together as you go through this text.

In struggle & solidarity,
Cristien Storm

INTRODUCTION

///////////////////////////////

I WAS THREE YEARS OLD WHEN I LEARNED HOW TO TAKE OFF THE FRILLY dresses my parents made me wear. I'd wait for them to leave the room, then yank the dress over my head and clumsily button up the white shirt that went with my favorite black, green, and purple wool plaid pantsuit with matching vest and cowboy boots. I loved that outfit. I felt fabulous in it. I'd clomp around in my pointy brown boots practicing my swagger. I hated, in contrast, the pastel dresses my parents would inevitably try to put me in. I was very clear on this. Checkered pantsuit with matching vest and cowboy boots—good. Dresses—bad. Simple. When I was little I knew exactly what I liked and didn't like. As I grew up, the world around me slowly eroded my confidence like an ocean chewing a sandy shoreline. I learned that boundaries, like shorelines, would be pounded on continuously by corrosive elements. I learned to negotiate a constantly changing perimeter. I learned that stability was like sand—consistent in its eternal shifting.

I grew up, like many people, without the fortune of being taught healthy communication skills. My models were a confusing and contradicting mess. I learned that children should be seen and not heard but adults yell all the time. I learned that crying means you are weak, but crying is also an effective way to get what you want. I learned that you never ask for things directly but resent people when they don't give you what you didn't ask for. I communicated in hesitant fits and starts, throwing words and wants out to the world in a desperate attempt to be understood without revealing too much about myself. When people didn't understand what I was saying, I would blame myself for not being clear or blame them for not being a good listener. I learned that communication was to be approached like a chess match. Use strategy and outwit your opponent. Communication was framed as a way to manipulate and manage the world and the people in it, not as a way to understand or listen. Communication was placed in a combative context. I struggled with this framework until I reached adulthood and eventually realized that communication is a relationship, not combat.

We all have individual experiences that shape how we learn to communicate our needs, wants, preferences, and limits. Each of us faces different obstacles or barriers to setting boundaries and we will be more adept at boundary setting in different situations depending on our experiences, values, and personality. Despite these differences, fear is a common response when people begin to identify and communicate needs. What we fear (anger, abandonment, punishment, missing out on something, etc.) depends on our personal narrative, but the motivation plays out the same: avoidance. Unfortunately, this is not an effective strategy. Fear is a powerful motivator but it inhibits communication. If we are afraid to identify what makes us happy and ask for it directly, we might try to ask indirectly. This hinting or sideways communication stops us from learning how to sit with the fear and anxiety of asking for what it is we truly want. Avoidance reinforces the belief that whatever it is we are avoiding should be avoided. Avoidance tricks us into deceiving ourselves. If we habitually communicate indirectly, we also risk losing sight of what we want and need. We link anxiety and our needs to the point where we may stop identifying our needs altogether because it creates an uncomfortable amount of anxiety. Our wants and needs are then defined by our avoidance of anxiety instead of a reflection of what they truly are.

Living like this often means we build a life with the scraps of what is left after we avoid, avoid, and avoid. Like a maze built from doors, you avoid one bad thing by going through a door and once that door shuts, the doors that are left determine your path. Our lives, our relationships, and our selves are defined by what is left rather than by who we are. Our true selves get buried under a mountain of fear. Instead of trying to avoid the anxiety and fear of asking for what we want, we can learn to tolerate and navigate the terrain of our anxiety. Most of us have an understanding of how powerful ocean waves are. If you have ever swum in the ocean, you know that when you get caught in an undertow, despite your initial response to swim madly for the shore, you have to relax and let the waves carry you. If you struggle, your risk of drowning is much higher than if you relax and let the waves pull you closer to shore where you can get your bearings. Fear and anxiety are like getting caught in a series of terrifying waves with a powerful undertow. Our first response is to thrash wildly. Our first response is natural, but it's not the most helpful. If you relax and let the waves come, ride them out rather than fight against them, they will pass and you can continue toward your goal. We can approach anxiety and fear like surfers who learn to override their initial urge to swim madly when caught inside powerful waves. Doing so helps us be more present. It's a matter of working with rather than struggling against what is happening. When you are not trying to avoid feelings or emotions, you are more connected to yourself and the present moment. And the more we connect with ourselves, the better we can connect to other people.

When we use boundaries to try to avoid fear and anxiety, we deny ourselves the opportunity to learn how to handle these emotions in healthier ways. We may fear being happy because we know it will go away, so we sabotage our joy. We may fear anger because we have been hurt by someone's anger, so we avoid anger at all costs. We may fear love because it has wounded us, so we snuff love out like a candle flame when it grows inside us. We fear getting fired because we are not sure how we would find another job. Our boundaries then become mechanisms to try to control other people, situations, and environments. For example, we don't set boundaries with our supervisor, so we set them with our partner because it feels safer; we say no to a desired relationship because it feels too scary to face the feelings that come up; we use boundaries to deny our frustration because it feels safer to direct it inward where it later manifests as illness or disease. There are times when we need to set these types of boundaries. We don't worry about whether or not we are avoiding fear or letting ourselves feel fear when we yank a child out of the way of a speeding bus. The problem arises when avoiding certain emotions becomes an automatic response across all situations. We then control our feelings in situations where it would benefit us to share them, and we may stop ourselves from exploring options or choices that could make us happy because they cause anxiety.

Environment and social context also inform boundaries. Growing up as a white middle-class woman I learned multilayered messages about power. I knew as a white woman I had some power, much more than many. I also learned there were times and places where, as a woman, I had very little power.

Years ago when I was just arriving on the doorstep of puberty, I witnessed a nasty argument between two married adults. The police were called. When the male police officer arrived, he deferred to the man, smiling and nodding sympathetically as he described the fight. He ignored the other woman and me, making sure to avoid all eye contact. The officer and the man walked past us into the living room side by side, casual, like buddies. I heard the officer ask, "Would you like to press charges, sir?" pointing to the scratches on the man's cheek and neck. "No, that's fine," he responded, nodding back at the officer. I saw him shake his head and smile at the officer. I saw the officer shake his head and smile back. They didn't need to translate. I got the message.

The officer turned to the woman after he and the man emerged from the living room. He stood over her, looming really. She was sobbing and having a hard time keeping herself together. The officer, in thick black boots, thick black utility belt, thick mustache, thick muscles, and a thick sneer, leaned toward her. She was barefoot in shorts and a T-shirt. She'd been cleaning. Her T-shirt was torn and stretched, exposing the length of her collarbone as it slid off one shoulder. "I don't see any bruises, ma'am, not much else we can do." It was true.

4

There were no visible bruises. Bruises, unlike (usually defensive) scratches, can sometimes take from one to three days to show up. She started to crumble. Shaking and crying, I remember her yelling at the cop, "Do you want to see what he did?" She tugged her T-shirt, yanking it up at the middle. I remember her bra was the same bright white as her shirt. The cop raised his hand, palm outstretched inches from her face: "Um, no ma'am that's not necessary." A sideways glace at the man. A slight purse of the lips. Pity. Anger. I'd learn much bigger words for it later in my UCSC Women's Studies courses. But that day, again, I got the message. As the cop left, he threw a backward glance at the woman and said directly and only to her, "I don't want to have to come back here. Let's not do anything stupid." There are times and there are places when you have very little power.

Long after the couple had made up, I carried the echo of that cop's words in my body: "Don't do anything stupid." I carried those words in my tightly held breath that fled to the corners of my lungs during the incident and stayed there in hiding for years. I continued to learn all the different ways we squash healthy communication and healthy boundaries. *What did she expect, wearing that? How many people has she slept with? What are you, a boy or a girl? You have such a nice face; you could be so pretty if you lost weight. What are you doing here? Don't you love me? If you loved me …* In other words, don't step out of line. Don't stray out of your place and role. And do not, under any circumstance, believe you have the right to define, establish, implement, and communicate any boundaries of your own. Like any good teenager, I rebelled.

I explored how to have boundaries in a world that taught me as a woman I should not have any. I got bigger and louder and more biting with my humor. I held men (and women) at bay with a razor-sharp tongue numbed with the accouterments of the young, the tough, the edgy, and the wounded. I thought these kinds of boundaries would keep me safe. They did not. I thought these kinds of boundaries would make me stronger, less vulnerable. Instead, they drained me and their rigidity restricted my sense of self. It was like wearing metal body armor. It's hard, solid, and dense. It's also cumbersome and weighs a ton. If you fall down, it is impossible to get back up with any kind of speed or grace. I decided after much clomping and trashing about in clumsy armor to try something else. I wanted to explore self-defense that wasn't rigid and made of metal. I wanted boundary setting that could be as malleable and as soft as a young sapling and just as strong as a deep-rooted tree. I didn't have a particular game plan, but the universe in its infinite wisdom provided me one.

In 1993, the rape and murder of a friend and fellow artist, Mia Zapata, changed my life and the lives of many of my friends and community members. In the aftermath of her murder, a group of us got together to figure out what to do with the pain and anger and fear and hopelessness we felt. In our conversations, ramblings, rants, and community dialogues we kept coming back to the idea of self-defense. We wanted self-defense that was accessible and met our needs. Our needs, as it turned out, were incredibly diverse. We founded Home Alive, an organization that attempted to hold all our diverging, and at times very contradictory, ideas of what self-defense and boundary setting were. Even while we acknowledged the complexity of safety and diversity of what people defined as violence, we struggled to not impose our values on others. It's hard. We want to be safe. We want others to be safe. When someone advocates something that seems "unsafe" from our frame of reference, it can be challenging to accept and support. Some people advocated the use of guns for personal and home protection, while other people's anti-violence values included an anti-gun stance. Home Alive addressed this by having gun safety classes and talking about weapons in workshops. Home Alive took the stance that there is no one "right way" to protect ourselves or set a boundary. We put self-defense within the context of human rights and supported other groups, organizations, and communities who were doing self-defense of their own. This included raising money for Mother's Against Police Brutality, a self-defense issue if ever there was one; organizing Seattle's annual Take Back The Night March when Seattle Rape Relief closed their doors; working with regional and international *antifa* (the European term referring to Anti-fascist individuals and groups that are dedicated to fighting fascism and white nationalism); creating self-defense and boundary-setting curriculums that addressed domestic violence; and supporting community organizing efforts of all kinds.

Home Alive created a space for me to explore, expand, and challenge ideas of how we defend ourselves and how we set boundaries. For over ten years I developed self-defense, anti-violence, and boundary-setting curriculums. I taught workshops for schools, prisons, non-profits, activists, lawyers, small businesses, radical anarchists, human rights coalitions, parents, and all kinds of other community members. I developed teacher trainings and spent most of my days (and a lot of my nights) talking about boundaries and boundary setting. During this time, I explored how to use self-defense and boundary-setting principles as methods for healing. I addressed my own trauma and wounds in a variety of ways. I did healing work as an individual and as a community member. As a writer and performer, I wrote, sang, and performed my healing. As a teacher, I brought the empowering and resilient sprit of survivors into every class. We focus so much on fear and how to avoid danger, that we often render invisible all the amazing things we are already doing, not only to survive but to thrive. In trying so hard to be safe, we miss out on life. We live in fear and fear of fear. It was exciting to reframe discussions of self-defense and boundary setting, to move from a fear-based orientation to a liberated mindset that cultivated a resilient, resourceful self-reliance rooted in community and self-care.

When I left Home Alive to work with The Northwest Coalition For Human Dignity (NWCHD) to do research and cultural organizing, I brought my enthusiasm for reframing discussions of violence and self-defense with me. NWCHD researched and monitored white nationalist activity in the Northwest and provided support for rural and suburban communities responding to bigotry and hate. Self-defense was a very important part of our work. The right to defend ourselves and protect others against bigotry and hate included a wide range of things. We supported individuals and communities who were responding to hate crimes, helped organizations counter the recruiting efforts of white nationalists, and defended people's right to live a life free from violence, hate, and discrimination. Again, I was surprised at how often we resorted to a fear-based framework that ignored or minimized the strength, tenacity, humor, wit, and resiliency of all those we worked with. Both of these organizations dealt with very violent, dark, and nasty aspects of society. It's not surprising that fear was a regular component of our work. We were repelled by it and compelled to respond to it in a constant shifting struggle to try to mitigate intense emotions. The drain and strain of this struggle was the collateral damage we all suffered. When I entered the next phase of my life as a mental health counselor, I took with me a deep desire to continue to find ways to counter fear and anxiety with hope and equanimity.

In my work as a therapist, boundary setting comes up all the time. I help people identify not only their needs, but also the barriers they face, and how the reality of their experience and environment informs what they will choose to do. Again and again, fear hops into the driver seat, peeling out before people even grasp what is going on. Before they know it, fear is whizzing them down a windy road and they are, so to speak, stuck in the passenger seat desperate to yank back the steering wheel and gain control but too afraid to do so. From where we want to eat to who we want to be in relationship with, to what our work life looks like, to how we feel about ourselves, boundaries inform and define almost every aspect of our lives. We can use boundaries to try to avoid fear and anxiety, or we can use them to create the kind of lives we want. *Empowered Boundaries* (formerly titled *Living in Liberation: Boundary Setting, Self-Care and Social Change*) challenges us to do the latter.

There are many books on boundaries. Most of them have good skills to share. What *Empowered Boundaries* offers that is unique is a simple, direct approach to boundaries and boundary setting that reflects the complexity of the world we live in while offering practical tools. This book looks deeply at how oppression (e.g., racism, classism, homophobia, transphobia, sexism, ableism, ageism) and privilege impact the context and interpersonal environments in which our boundary setting occurs.

In all the years I have been teaching and talking about boundary setting, I keep coming back to the same principles over and over. This text offers them for you to explore. The scenarios, examples, and quotations included in this work are amalgamations from years of teaching classes, workshops, and my therapy work. They are not based on any one person or situation and serve to illuminate themes that many people struggle with rather than any one particular experience. Please take what works for you, leave what doesn't, and share what gets you excited with family and friends. I hope you enjoy this book. I hope you find it helpful, and I hope it supports your work in negotiating and creating the things you want in your life.

PART I

ONE

WHAT IS A BOUNDARY?

A BOUNDARY INVOLVES ESTABLISHING OR NEGOTIATING HOW WE ARE IN our environments and relationships. Boundaries are informed by our experiences in the world and the responses we get from others. This includes our family dynamics, the intergenerational history of our families and communities, the social systems we do or do not have access to, the institutions we navigate, our personalities, our sense of who we are in the world, the power and privilege we have or can access, and our lived experiences. Boundaries change and grow, expand and contract alongside the aspects of our emotional, physical, mental, and spiritual self. Boundaries make up who we are and play a role in how we are who we are.

Boundaries are our way of communicating what we want and don't want, what we need and don't need. Some boundaries come instinctually, like yelling out in fright. Other boundaries are learned, like how to say no to an unwanted request, or ask for what we need in an effective way. When I facilitate boundary-setting workshops I ask participants for their definition(s) of a boundary. In classes, I get all sorts of responses. Definitions like a bubble, a limit, a line, your personal space, or your right to say no. Examples of how to express a boundary have included "Please don't talk to me like that," "Don't touch me," "Leave me alone," "Go away," and "No." People rarely offer definitions that involve bringing people closer, letting people in, or asking people what it is they want. Examples could include: "I would really like you to give me a hug," "Can you sit next to me rather than across from me when we talk?," "Please touch me like this," "I would like you to be closer to me," and "Yes."

When we think of boundary setting, we tend to think of the word "No." We connect our perception of a strong boundary with someone's ability to say no clearly and in no uncertain terms. Saying no is a powerful thing. Being able to say no can liberate and empower us tremendously. Saying no, however, is also only one part of the entire boundary-setting picture. Boundaries are as much about saying yes as they are about saying no. Building holistic, healthy, and happy relationships and lives includes both identifying (and asking for or working toward) what we want and what we do not want. Being able to state clearly and directly what we don't want is important. There will be times when this is the only relevant thing we want to communicate. If I am being harassed at a club, I might tell the person, "I don't want to talk to you," or, "I don't want you to touch me." I may, however, choose to tell them what I *do* want, for example, by saying, "Leave me alone" or "I want you to go away." There will be times when we will care very much about telling someone what we want. It may be important to share with a friend how they can support you by explaining specifically what you want or need, for example. Telling someone what *not* to do, is not, by definition, telling them what to do.

It can be hard, for a variety of reasons, to tell someone what you want. Sometimes we don't know. Fear and reactivity can complicate identifying and communicating what we want or need. If we do not feel safe, feel threatened or anxious it may be safer to state what we do not want. The United States perpetuates a culture of fear in many ways through media and messaging about safety, self-defense, and self-care. We will explore this more in chapter six, but for now, it is important to begin to consider how fear and reactivity inform boundaries by pushing us to focus on what we don't want. While stating what we do not want is not inherently bad, there are times when stating things in terms of what we do want allows for more information to be communicated and allows for more creative problem-solving about how to make it happen. For example, I don't want global warming, child abuse, or economic disparity, among other things. How can I express these wants in non-reactionary terms that qualify what I would like to happen? "I want an international community that respects our planet above economic gains." "I want loving and supportive families made of individuals that come from loving and supportive families that are supported by loving and supportive communities." "I want to interweave our economic stability to the economic justice and the health and well-being of every person in our country." These are just some examples of how to reframe statements of needs or wants. Reframing asks us not only to consider what we want; it asks us to envision possibilities and even strategies for obtaining our goals. This (sometimes counterintuitively) can be scary and even painful. Identifying, asking for, and envisioning getting what we want offers hope, but it is also rooted in the reality of what is, which is sometimes painful to consider.

Asking for what we want requires that we have a clear vision of what we want (or at least a fuzzy outline). It can be challenging and even frightening to reflect deeply on what it is that we want and then imagine communicating that with the people in our lives. It can feel vulnerable and at times overwhelmingly terrifying, especially when the stakes are high and the outcome matters. It may feel safer to not ask at all, as hearing a refusal or not having our request met with compassion can be painful and we may not feel equipped to handle it. Communicating what we want can be incredibly challenging when it involves making (sometimes very personal) requests to people, or in situations where asking means taking a chance or being vulnerable, or when power is not equitable. Identifying what we want might be connected to past traumatic events that make communicating it seem overwhelming or even impossible.

*I lived my life trying to prevent what had happened from happening
again. I lived by default and saw danger everywhere. I was not living,
I was trying not to get hurt or die—an impossibility if you are on this
planet. When I gave up trying to prevent things from occurring and
dealing with life as it was, I began living and I learned to trust myself.
I learned that I could not control other people or events but that my fear
had struggled against this reality. When I accepted this, I accepted my
own power and my own strengths.*

—HOME ALIVE BOUNDARY-SETTING CLASS PARTICIPANT

Fear of exploring and communicating what we want can cause anxiety. We may try to avoid this anxiety by avoiding setting or negotiating boundaries altogether. People can spend a great deal of time constructing their lives and relationships so as to avoid setting boundaries as much as possible. This costs us not only time and energy, it costs us the full potential of our relationships and ourselves. We can't be fully present when we are operating out of anxiety or fear.

Knowing what we want and need, and being able to communicate it, not only benefits us, it also helps those on the receiving end of our boundaries. Think about it. Isn't it helpful to know what is expected or desired of you, even if you don't necessarily want to do it? It is much easier to follow a request to not do something when it is followed by what you can do. It also softens the boundary. There are times when we may not want or need to provide information about what the person can do or soften a boundary in any way. In other situations, it may be important for us that the other person understands what we want and also be able to do it. Context is everything.

Saying what we want can also be a way of providing an alternative: *This* is not helpful but *this* would be. It may involve telling our partner that we don't want them to offer advice when we are telling them about our day, but would prefer they just listen. It could be yelling at a stranger who grabs your arm at a party that you don't like to be grabbed and to let go of your arm, *Now!* We might offer our child the option of having a healthy treat after denying them a candy bar. In past boundary-setting classes, participants have sometimes expressed concern that providing an alternative is about trying to lessen guilt or mitigate anxiety about setting a boundary, and that we need to learn how to say no without feeling guilty. Saying no without feeling guilty is a worthy goal and something most of us can work on. Offering an alternative or stating what we want is one of many boundary-setting skills that we will explore further in this book, and while there may be times when we do it out of guilt (which is not inherently bad), there will be other times when we are invested in telling someone what we want them to do. In classes, we practice a variety of skills in a number of different contexts. There will be times when it is scary to say no without justifying, explaining, or defending our boundary, and our work is to learn how to increase our capacity to not act out of guilt but to firmly hold onto our boundary without explanation. Setting a boundary without justifying it or having to offer an alternative is a vital skill. It is just as vital to learn how to tell people what we want, how to say yes. Both are important boundary-setting skills.

We set boundaries all the time. Some are emotionally fairly neutral, like saying "No, thanks" to a refill of coffee. Others are more highly charged, like ending a relationship. Who we are informs not only with whom we set boundaries, but also informs how and why we set boundaries. For many of us, setting and negotiating boundaries is foreign territory. We were told that having boundaries is bad so we learned to ignore or avoid them. We might have learned that we only get to have boundaries if we fight for them, and therefore have to be ready to defend or give up any boundary we may have dared try to set if we "lose." It takes a lot of energy to battle over boundaries. Battling puts us in a defensive position and we can end up approaching boundary setting like a debate. Boundaries are not a debate. Boundaries can be negotiated, discussed, investigated, reflected upon, but not debated. We should not have to "win" the right to our boundaries. Nor should we have to verify the necessity or authenticity of our boundaries with a more "logical" argument.

When boundary setting is approached like a debate, it suggests that one's right to boundaries has to be proved. This also suggests that without "proof" there should be no boundary. This strategy embodies the myth that by hearing both sides, we arrive at an objective truth. Boundaries are not objective. They are subjective. There are times when one person feels like they have a right to set a boundary in a specific situation and someone else may disagree. You may believe that it is perfectly acceptable to tell a friend you don't want to hug them, while someone else believes that it is not only a bad boundary, but even rude behavior. If we approach a situation such as this like a debate, we would hear both sides and then decide who was "right." This makes our right to a boundary conditional. We don't need to prove our right to a boundary. Our right to our boundaries is not conditional.

If we buy into this debate-oriented approach, we often spend grand amounts of time and energy prepping our defenses. By the time we attempt to communicate a boundary, we are already prepared to be defensive. We have anticipated every variable, strategized every angle, worked over solutions to every possible scenario, constructed counter arguments and engineered excuses. Preparing for battle makes us rigid, tense, and inflexible. We imagine that our boundaries, like walls or arguments, are better and stronger when they are solid, sturdy, thick, and impenetrable. Sometimes this is true. Sometimes it is not. Sometimes the best wall (or argument, or boundary) is porous and flexible. Again, context is everything.

Boundaries are informed by the social context in which we live, which in turn is deeply informed by the amount of privilege we have (or don't have), and the systems of oppression that operate in our society. I once participated in self-defense classes for women and learned a great many things on the day we covered boundary setting. The facilitator, a bright-eyed and chipper young white woman with college-educated speech, tidy loafers, and a matching sweat suit, started off the session by explaining how you could set a boundary simply with the words you choose. You could, for example, swear: "You can say the S-word or the F-word," she told us. She then went on to explain that since people wouldn't expect this from you, you could "buy time" because your attacker would be shocked from your choice of words. I was shocked. Not because the facilitator said, "Fuck off!" as an example, but because she thought it was shocking. The community I live in uses the F-word like grammatical glue. Saying "Fuck" would not be shocking. How you say it could emphasize your point and set a clear boundary. The word itself, however, would not faze most of the people I lived and worked with at the time. Clearly she was not from my world. This is a small example of how we need to customize the tools we use to fit the social context, rather than use a one-size-fits-all approach. Remember the definition at the beginning of this section? We will all negotiate our lives, our relationships, and our safety differently. Different tools work better for different people. We will use different tools at different times and our toolbox will continue to change and evolve.

Self-defense as a women's empowerment concept has been predominantly tailored to white middle-class women. Although there are numerous examples of self-defense as a community framework, such as the Black Panther Party for Self-Defense, the Center For Anti-Violence Education, and the Worker Defense Campaign led by the employees of Zanon ceramic tile factory, the mainstream concept of self-defense still remains predominately rooted in white middle-class fears of danger and white middle-class definitions of safety. These concepts of self-defense and boundary setting are rooted in the early feminist movements that strove to address rape, sexual assault, and violence against women, among other things. These movements, which encapsulated white privilege in the ways victims were identified, the ways safety was defined, and the ways in which perpetrators were punished, have a history of inaccessibility for marginalized communities, including queer and trans folks, men and women of color, those with differing abilities and financially-poor men and women, among many others whose lived experiences were neither reflected nor represented equitably. When I asked the facilitator of my self-defense class, "So, what if the context in which you live is one where language like that isn't shocking?" I was informed that "using the F-word" was a strong indicator of how upset you were in any context. Okay, but even if I put "the F-word" in my boundary-setting tool belt, it still felt light. I wanted to add some weight to it.

I don't mean to speak badly of mainstream self-defense and boundary-setting trainings for women. They offer invaluable skills and have saved many lives. But women's self-defense and boundary-setting curriculums are still too often rooted in privilege. More mainstream curriculums do not typically address the kinds of violence that many people must defend themselves from: police brutality, abuse by border control vigilantes, corporate decimation of the planet, hate crimes, Three Strikes laws that target and incarcerate poor men of color in incredibly disproportionate rates, forced sterilization programs like CRACK (Children Requiring a Caring Kommunity),[4] or other barriers to accessing health care. Comparing hate crimes to limited access to health care may seem like a stretch, but the people whose lives are severely impacted by a lack of quality health and medical care might disagree. Focusing on individual violence without placing it in a larger social context is primarily a privilege for those whose lives (and bodies) are already healthy, safe, comfortable, and taken care of. If you cannot access quality health care, or any care at all, because your life or body are not seen as valuable, you are being victimized in ways that people in other communities are not.

Consider the following example: a single parent cannot get mental health support for their child and they lose their job because they are forced to manage their child's health care alone. They in turn lose their home because they are unemployed and have to file bankruptcy because they cannot afford medications and food, and they themselves eventually suffer medical conditions from the chronic stress and fatigue after years of struggling with homelessness and unemployment (which they can't afford to treat). Due to all these circumstances they may believe (and I would agree) that what they experienced is very much a form of

---

[4]   CRACK is a private nonprofit organization that offers a $200 cash incentive primarily to women of color struggling with drug abuse and addiction to drugs or alcohol in an attempt to persuade them to undergo sterilization or get long-acting contraceptive methods such as hormone injections, implants, or IUDs.

violence. This scenario, unfortunately, is all too common. When we talk about self-defense or boundary setting, what tends to get prioritized is individual safety. Individual safety isn't a bad thing; it just excludes the violence that many communities are grappling with. For some communities, being able to defend against systemic or institutional violence is just as important as defending against individual violence. Individual safety-oriented programs, in focusing on individual violence and safety, also ignore the self-defense these communities are already doing and the creative ways in which they take care of each other.

When we say that boundaries are a negotiation of how we are in our environments, we need to take these environments into account. My self-defense cohort thought that yelling "Fuck" was a fabulous tool because it would startle the people (men) in our environment. If I tried to bring this tool to a group of young women who were not white, middle/upper class, college educated, primarily straight, able bodied, and over eighteen years old, it would look much different. Try telling a group of fifteen-year-old refugee girls from Cambodia to "just yell 'Fuck you'" at their attacker or telling it to a multiethnic group of gay men, an African American youth church group, or a punk rock collective of vegan anarchists. You get the idea. The point is not to substitute a different word or skill for "the F-word," but to look at how easily examples of boundary setting can embody oppressive systems if we're not careful in both our critique and construction of them.

Boundaries are the negotiation of how we are in our environments and relationships. How we do this and what we look like while doing it varies from person to person and relationship to relationship. We might use the same tools; we might not. Our tools, like our tool belts, will reflect who we are in all our glorious individuality. We could choose a no-nonsense tool belt, a fanny pack, a green felt purse, a silver cigarette holder-cum-wallet, a faux alligator skin suitcase, the pocket of our baggy jeans, a bike messenger bag with a picture of Elvis on it, a fuzzy blue backpack, or pink furry carryall. Whatever it is, I hope it gets a little heavier as you read on. In the next part, we look at some tools we can use to set boundaries.

TWO

LEARNING TO SET BOUNDARIES

IN MY WORK WITH GROUPS ON SETTING AND MAINTAINING BOUNDARIES, I've found four tools to be effective. All of them are based on learning and strengthening communication skills and are categorized under the following titles: NAME THE BEHAVIOR, GIVE A DIRECTIVE, BROKEN RECORD, and END AN INTERACTION. The tools themselves are not new and many different groups teach them. Sometimes, however, these tools are taught in a way that reflects the idea that boundaries are always about keeping people out, saying no, and putting up walls. My view is that these tools are also effective when we use them to practice negotiating what we want. Learning to say yes is just as much a part of boundary setting as learning to say no.

NAME THE BEHAVIOR

There are a lot of reasons boundaries get crossed. People cross our boundaries simply because they choose to cross them, irrespective of what we want, or due to miscommunication, confusion, different wants and needs, power imbalances, abuse, and finally, violence. Before you can respond, you have to know that it's possible to set a boundary, that you have a right to set one, and you have to be aware of when the boundary has been crossed. A great deal of boundary setting is done with people we care about and with whom we will continue to negotiate a relationship. This complicates boundary work, as boundaries may be at odds with maintaining relationships.

NAME THE BEHAVIOR entails clearly stating what behavior(s) will be addressed or negotiated. "You are yelling at me." "You keep trying to kiss me." "You are standing really close to me." "You continue to call me after I told you to stop." "When I say yes to one thing, you continue to ask for more." "It seems you expect me to work late every day." "When I come home later than expected, you get upset even if I call." "When I ask you to spend more time with me, I feel like you ignore my request." Stating the behavior can clarify specific behaviors that will be addressed through boundary setting. Interpersonal interactions are often complicated and sometimes it is helpful to use NAME THE BEHAVIOR as an internal, personal exercise to help sort through what is important to address. Other times, it may be helpful to name the behavior to a support system, get feedback on the situation or interaction, and explore possible responses to any identified boundary crossings. It is also possible to use NAME THE BEHAVIOR to identify concerns that need to be addressed after building or increasing a support system. I have worked with survivors of domestic violence, for example, who realized their relationship was abusive long before they were ready or able to name particular behaviors and leave the relationship. One survivor in a boundary-setting workshop shares how she used the NAME THE BEHAVIOR skill:

After a while, I began to realize that no matter what I did, my partner would be jealous and blame me. It always ended up being my fault somehow. I think that when I finally said this out loud to myself one night after an argument, I realized how bad it was. I finally understood that this wasn't about whether I worked late, or talked too much to someone at a party, that there would always be a reason to blame me. I think naming the behavior helped me begin the process of asking for support and eventually leaving the relationship.

24

The above scenario is a good example of how to first name the behavior to yourself and then to a support system before ever telling the person with whom you are setting the boundary. In this instance, she made her decision based on her own emotional well-being and for safety reasons.

A co-facilitator in another class shares an example of a different way of using NAME THE BEHAVIOR:

I was on a first date with someone who I had just met. We were talking at a café and at some point she put her hand on my leg, flirting with me. I didn't feel threatened or anything, but I wasn't really into the date, so I made a joke about how it was too early for that kind of touch and shifted away a bit. She laughed and took her hand away, but a few minutes later, she put it back again, casually, while telling me a story. Reflecting on it now, I remember thinking that she was pushy. I still didn't feel intimidated or threatened or anything. I just moved again and told her I had a nice time but that I had to go and I left. I never called her and she didn't call me.

This person chose to name the behavior in her own head and to not say anything aloud to her date for a few reasons. She first took stock and decided she was not that invested in maintaining the relationship; she didn't feel unsafe or threatened and, she made a plan to keep using the boundary skills she was already employing (i.e., body language, removing her date's hand, humor, resituating herself) and ended the date early. This is another example of how to use NAME THE BEHAVIOR nonverbally.

People are sometimes concerned that using NAME THE BEHAVIOR nonverbally is actually just avoiding boundary setting altogether. It depends on intention and context. If someone believes they do not have the right, or is not sure how to set a boundary or name a behavior directly to someone, then the issue may be about avoiding boundary setting. If someone does not have the skill, capacity, or feels it is not safe to tell a person directly, the decision may be strategically sound. Often, people come to boundary-setting workshops with few models of how to identify and set boundaries. They enter class with the goal of learning life skills that they can bring to their relationships and interactions. Sometimes the first skill is learning that setting a boundary is possible and that it may involve many steps that help prepare people for the act of stating a boundary directly. In some cases, pointing out a boundary crossing or telling someone directly that what they did crossed a boundary can lead to victim-blaming, shaming, threats, intimidation, and even physical danger. When I first began to develop boundary-setting curriculums with other Home Alive instructors, we discussed the complexities of teaching workshops for people who have experienced (or who were currently surviving) domestic violence. In classes, many people (including those who had experienced domestic violence) expressed relief in knowing that naming the behavior to oneself was an actual skill. One survivor shares her thoughts:

I was afraid that if I said anything, he would get mad. Even though I knew it was not okay that he was threatening me. When I told him that what he was doing was wrong or manipulative or even abusive, he would tell me I didn't know what I was talking about and that I didn't understand how I was pushing him to the point where the only thing he could do was yell or break things. No matter how I tried to point out that what he was doing was wrong, it seemed like it always came back to me. I stopped telling him what I thought. I shut down and began to think about out how to get out of there rather than how to try to change. I didn't stop seeing his behaviors. In fact pointing it out to myself made me feel less crazy. It's cool to hear that me naming the behavior to myself was a way of setting boundaries. You blame yourself for staying, for putting up with it, and it is hard to see what you did do.

Of course, there are times when one will name the behavior very clearly and out loud and to other people. A friend of mine shared a story with me. She was taking the New York City subway. She was alone and on her way to meet someone for dinner. The train was packed tight with commuters. As she stood jammed between people clinging to the pole by the exit doors, she felt a hand on her right butt cheek. She froze, thinking, *is that a hand on my ass?* She waited a few seconds and confirmed—yep, that was a hand on her ass. She looked around and the hand disappeared. After a few beats it was back. *Shit, this time he's even grabbier,* she thought. She turned slowly and out of the corner of her eye identified the man who was grabbing her. "Oh my God, you're grabbing my butt! Did you all see that?" she yelled, looking at him and then around at everyone on the train. People looked away or down, not wanting to get involved. My friend was undeterred. She looked directly at the man, then at everyone around her, yelling, "I can't believe you grabbed my ass! You grab women's butts on the train!" She kept it up until, agitated and looking down, the man got off the train. As he exited, she popped her head through the closing train doors and yelled after him, "Watch out everyone, that man right there in the blue jacket, he grabs women's butts on the train." People glanced at him curiously and continued on their way. Clearly, my friend could explicitly name the behavior.

It is normal to try to anticipate the other person's response when we name the behavior. Class participants have asked me all kinds of questions about the impact of using NAME THE BEHAVIOR. "What do I do if someone responds in a way that I don't like?" "What if they get angry?" "What if use NAME THE BEHAVIOR and I hurt their feelings? Or offend them?" "Can't NAME THE BEHAVIOR be rude or escalate things?" One of most important aspects of these tools is being able to choose when and how to use them. Ultimately, we have no control over how other people will respond to a boundary. While we might know our family member or partner's buttons, and can impact and influence the people in our lives at times, they are ultimately the ones who choose how they will respond. Of course, interpersonal interactions are complicated by individual experiences, histories of trauma and abuse, power, privilege, and other social factors that inform how one will respond in a situation.

There may be times when naming the behavior can, in fact, escalate a situation. This is not always bad. There are times when escalating things is helpful. A client of mine discussed how he was afraid of conflict. He would avoid everything he saw as a potential conflict to the detriment of himself and his relationships. As we addressed his fears, he began to engage in, rather than always avoid, conflicts. This involved having conversations that became heated, agitated, and at times escalated. As his capacity to feel anxious and engage in (rather than avoid) disagreements increased, the possibility of conflict became much less scary and he was able to identify, negotiate, and set more boundaries.

VICTIM BLAMING

The concern that naming the behavior will escalate an interaction is often tied to the belief that those setting the boundary are also responsible for how the other person responds. That if someone sets a boundary in a certain (or correct) way, they will get a specific result. While it is true that people may be aware of what will agitate someone or make them feel upset or hurt, the concept of being responsible for how someone responds is rooted, in part, in the culture of victim blaming. Victim blaming not only places responsibility on the boundary setter for how someone reacts, it takes the focus off the other person and their behavior. There are many ways victim blaming plays out. Women experience victim blaming when society sends the message that women control the way men act. From wearing provocative clothing that "causes" rape, to acting "crazy" in ways that "made" someone hit them, women get the message that they are responsible for other people's behaviors. Survivors of bullying and hate crimes are often made to feel as if it is their fault, that they were targeted because they looked or acted differently than what was perceived as the "correct" way, or because who they are represents a supposed "threat" or danger. Victim blaming can lead people to try to figure out the "right" boundary skill that will "cause" a particular reaction. In boundary-setting classes, people ask all the time, "How do I use NAME THE BEHAVIOR in a way that won't upset or hurt someone?" or "How do I use NAME

THE BEHAVIOR in a way that makes the person respect my boundary?" While you can be mindful about how you are using the skill and be reflective on what you know about effective communication with a particular person, as mentioned previously, you can't control how they will respond. You can only choose how you respond to their response.

Sometimes it is not clear in the moment whether a boundary has been crossed. If it is clear that a boundary has been crossed, it can be challenging to come up with a response on the spot. Practicing NAME THE BEHAVIOR not only helps one get clear on what behaviors need to be addressed, but also offers one a chance to imagine a variety of creative responses. It can be helpful to play around and try out new behaviors. In classes, I encourage participants to role-play different ways of naming the behavior. If someone is shy and quiet, I might encourage them to practice being loud and assertive to see what it feels like. If someone is highly verbal, I may encourage them to practice using only body language to name the behavior. If someone is anxious about a particular response, I may encourage them to practice NAME THE BEHAVIOR in low-stakes scenarios. For example, one class participant shared that she became very anxious when she thought she might disappoint someone. We role-played low-stakes situations where she got to name the behavior that entailed telling a waiter the order she received was incorrect. Practice can also involve recalling past situations and imaging or role-playing what you would have liked to say or how you would have liked to respond.

FREEZE FRAMING

Sometimes it is not immediately clear what behavior needs to be named. When it is unclear, it can be helpful to roll things backwards. Like freeze-framing a movie, the idea is to recall an event or interaction and then stop at each "frame" and examine it. What is happening in this moment? What behaviors are occurring? Who is doing what? What is being said? Do the behaviors sync with what is being said?

What thoughts, feelings, sensations, and action urges are present for me? If no boundary crossing is identified in the "frame," then roll it back to the previous frame and examine that moment until it becomes clear where or how a boundary was crossed. Sometimes no matter how many times the movie is replayed, what happened or where the boundary was crossed still remains unclear. When this occurs, it can be helpful to name thoughts, sensations, feelings, action urges, somatic responses, or even the uncertainty itself, just as one would name the behavior. An example might be, "I do not know what boundary was crossed, but I sense that one was." Or, "It is unclear how this person made me feel like they crossed a boundary, but they did and it is important to pay attention to that." Or, "I felt nervous, my hands clenched, and I wanted to leave." Being able to name an experience and decide how to respond, even if one is unable to point to an exact boundary crossing, is an important part of boundary setting. There are situations where events and interactions are unclear or confusing. This does not mean that one cannot use NAME THE BEHAVIOR as a boundary-setting tool.

Naming the behavior in clear, direct, nonjudgmental language that is focused on facts is key. Saying, "She was totally rude" does not identify the problem as clearly as saying, "She continued to ask me to work for her even after I told her I couldn't." The second statement focuses on the facts of the situation and is free of judgment, which makes identifying both the behavior and the potential boundary one might want to set in response much easier. Communicating in terms of facts and behaviors also makes it more likely that the other person will understand and comply. It's easier to change a behavior if one doesn't feel judged. Judgment often provokes defensiveness, which in turn can provoke even more defensiveness from the other person. Mutual defensiveness can lead to a power struggle with both people trying to prove why they or their behavior are right. Rather than exploring one another's perspectives or trying to understand the boundary, a power struggle entrenches people in justifying their perspective, often at the expense of being able to listen to the other person. While explaining nonjudgmentally what boundary was crossed is not a guarantee for successful communication, it is almost always preferable because it improves the chances that the other person will hear what you are naming. Taking the time to name the behavior without judgment or name-calling creates conditions in which it is easier to hear the concern. This also applies when we are naming the behavior to ourselves and to our support systems. Naming nonjudgmentally helps identify and clarify in ways that judgments often impede.

Being able to name the behavior is critical to boundary setting. Play around with this skill in low-risk situations that are not highly emotional. The more you practice, the more skilled you will become. Like developing any skill, it's easier to learn by beginning in low-stress environments and then move on to more challenging situations after gaining mastery and feeling more confident and comfortable.

GIVE A DIRECTIVE

The second skill is GIVE A DIRECTIVE. This entails telling the person what to do. In my experience, this tool is taught mostly as a command term—that is, telling people to stop a behavior that you don't want. While this is important, I also want to include how to give what I call a "Positive Directive" in our discussion—that is, a directive for what you would like the person to do or start doing. The term Positive Directive does not imply that the commanding directive is negative; they are not opposites but rather different tools we will choose to use at different times. Positive directives provide an alternative by telling someone what they can do, which often reduces resistance to the boundary. GIVE A DIRECTIVE, like NAME THE BEHAVIOR, may also be an internal experience. You can name the behavior to yourself: *She is ignoring that I just said no and trying to talk me into loaning her money again.* Then give a directive to yourself: *Just hold steady, don't get pulled in by her ability to hook me emotionally. I don't need to feel guilty.* Then you could simply set the boundary by saying, "No." Or the experience could be external.

You could, for example, explicitly tell someone, "You are yelling at me" (NAME THE BEHAVIOR). "I'll talk to you about this when you can talk to me without raising your voice" (GIVE A DIRECTIVE). This is an example of a Positive Directive. An example of a Command Directive would be one that does not offer an alternative: "You are yelling at me. Stop yelling at me."

Take a moment to think about times when a Command Directive might be a good choice and when a Positive Directive might work better. There is no right or wrong answer. It will be different for everyone. It's important to be able to choose how and when to set boundaries and offer directives. Rather than seeking a formula for boundary setting, it can be helpful to have options that are flexible and adaptable to different contexts. For example, a boundary may be set differently with a coworker who interrupts a conversation than with a stranger at a music club. Positive directives can "soften the blow," diffuse defensiveness, and redirect by offering someone something that they can do.

The directive, like NAME THE BEHAVIOR, is often more effective if it's free of judgment, blaming, shaming, interpretation, or "meaning-making." Meaning-making involves attaching a particular value or significance to a behavior. For example, telling someone, "You are twenty minutes late (NAME THE BEHAVIOR) ... you are inconsiderate (judgment) ... you being late lets me know you don't care about me (meaning-making) ... you need to be on time (Command Directive)" may elicit defensiveness about whether or not the other person really is inconsiderate or whether or not it is true that they do not consider your feelings. While there is no guarantee of how people will respond, a statement that is focused on sharing feelings, and that is free of judgment, shaming, and meaning-making may elicit less defensive reactions. Consider a different statement: "You are twenty minutes late (NAME THE BEHAVIOR) ... I am feeling hurt and frustrated. I was looking forward to our time together (sharing feelings) ... I really want you to try to be on time when we make plans (Positive Directive)... " The goal is not to make sure our directives are always free of judgment or to come up with the "perfect" directive. The goal is to have a variety of options and to be intentional about choosing when and how to name the behavior or give a directive.

The section below builds on examples of naming the behavior and illustrates ways to give a directive. Each example begins with naming the behavior, then includes a Positive Directive and a Command Directive. It is important to remember that the context informs the boundary work. These statements are examples without much context. Imagine different contexts and think about different ways these scenarios may look. You might imagine using different tones, body language, volume, word choice, etc. depending on the context.

— EXAMPLES —

You are yelling at me. I'll address your concerns once you can talk to me without raising your voice. Stop yelling at me right now!

You keep trying to kiss me after I have said I don't want you to. Don't do that anymore. Stop it. I'd feel more comfortable kissing you after we've spent more time together. I'm not into kissing right now, but I'd love to sit and cuddle with you on the couch.

You are standing really close to me. It makes me feel uncomfortable, can you take a step back, please. You are standing too close to me. Back off. (Notice that this example includes what could be a question, but the punctuation is a period. This is because it is not a question; it's a statement. It could also read: Please take a step back. Some people do not like using the word *Please* when giving a directive. This is a personal choice and demonstrates how different people will use different ways of setting boundaries in different contexts.)

You keep calling my house when I've asked you to stop. Don't call me anymore. If I am ready to be in contact, I will let you know.

When I say yes to one thing, you continue to ask for more. I'd like to be able to say yes without you asking for more. When I say yes to one thing, I would like it if you respect that by not asking for anything else. No.

It's seems like you expect me to work late every day. I can't work late every day. I can stay late on Wednesday and Thursday but that's my limit. I'd like to get clarity on your expectations for me. I am unable to meet your expectations.

BROKEN RECORD

BROKEN RECORD, as the name implies, is repeating the directive over and over as necessary. There are a few ways this tool can be effective. Through using the BROKEN RECORD strategy, you can interrupt explaining, justifying, or defending a boundary. Explaining, justifying, or defending a boundary can be distracting, emotionally and physically draining, and/or weaken your resolve. If someone is so busy explaining why a boundary is valid, they may not be aware of how their boundary is being chipped away at. Or, if a person is defending a boundary and can't come up with a reason why their boundary is "good" or reasonable, they may not know how to maintain it. Challenging a boundary is important and not necessarily bad or wrong, but it can be difficult to feel entitled to a boundary when it has been challenged, or if the reasons for wanting or needing the boundary are unclear to the other person (or sometimes even unclear to the person setting the boundary). It is important to separate the boundary itself from the ability to explain, justify, or defend it. Acting like a broken record can help people do this because the person can simply repeat the boundary or directive in response to a challenge, a question, or when they realize they are being pulled into explaining or justifying a boundary and they don't want to. For example, if you tell your daughter that she cannot go to a concert, it is within the realm of possibility that she will ask why or challenge your reasoning. While it may be important to give an explanation, the broken record helps ground the boundary. The parent can offer reasons and justifications (that the daughter will most likely attempt to demonstrate as unreasonable) while repeating the boundary. It can also allow people to offer compassion, empathy, or understanding without feeling as if these things undermine their boundary. "I know it's really hard that I won't let you go to a concert." "I can see that me refusing to go with you to your work party is upsetting." "I am really sorry that you are disappointed that I won't talk to you about this." "I get it that you are angry, and my answer is still 'No.'"

Repeating a directive can also help keep focus on what the other person is *doing* in response to a boundary, rather than on defending, explaining, or justifying said boundary. Being aware of what the other person is saying and doing informs how one responds to the other person's response to the boundary. The person might be saying one thing and doing another, which is helpful to recognize. For example, a person may say they understand a boundary but ask questions in a manner that feels like an attempt to discredit it. Or, someone may acknowledge the boundary and then proceed to ignore it. Directing attention to what is happening rather than justifying a boundary also cultivates awareness of triggers and hooks. Hooks, in this context, are the words, behaviors, actions and responses that prompt someone to give up or change a boundary. Pushback in response to a boundary is part of interpersonal relationships and in and of itself is not bad or good. When someone has set a boundary that we don't want, all of us have looked for loopholes or ways to push back against the boundary. Whether it's asking a friend for a ride to a party that you really really want to go to even though you know they are not that interested in attending, or asking more than once to borrow your sister's shoes (that she never wears and that you love), or asking your partner to justify why they refuse to spend their savings on a vacation, or demanding an explanation of why the bus driver can't let you off in between stops when it's pouring rain. Whatever it is, at some point we have all pushed back when confronted with a boundary. It's normal. It's human nature and it is to be expected. The BROKEN RECORD strategy can be extremely helpful in negotiating pushback. Just as with GIVE A DIRECTIVE, the broken record can be softened with alternatives: "I can't work late tonight, but I can on Wednesdays"; "I don't want to walk back with you, but I'll wait with you until you find someone who does"; "I won't have this conversation right now, but I will tomorrow afternoon." It can also be softened with affirmations or acknowledgment of feelings: "I'm looking forward to hanging out and even though I can't tonight, I'm excited to figure out a time next week"; "I appreciate your enthusiasm and it would be really helpful for me if you didn't interrupt me until I'm done sharing"; "I'm sorry but that won't work for me"; "I know it is difficult for you when I work late, let's make sure to spend quality time together this week"; "Thank you for understanding my need for this boundary, I can see it's challenging for you." Of course, there are times when we don't want or need to soften our boundary. There may be times when being the broken record simply entails saying "No" over and over again.

END AN INTERACTION

The final skill is called END AN INTERACTION. This skill may be used to stop a conversation, finish an interaction, leave a situation, or sever a relationship. This may be done even if things are not resolved and even if the other person does not want things to end. Again, context is important. Some people have no trouble ending a conversation or walking away. Other people may have no idea how to end a discussion or even a relationship that they no longer want to be in. A person's response to attempts to end things, and one's reaction to their responses are also important to consider. Getting to know yourself, your hooks, and the context in which boundary-setting skills are more or less challenging is part of boundary work. Understanding why you may be able to set clear limits or end an interaction in some situations but not others is important. Likewise, identifying how we respond to people's reactions to a boundary is part of boundary work. One can end an interaction verbally and nonverbally. Just as with the other boundary-setting skills, people will use different word choice, tones, volume, body language, gestures, facial expressions, and other communication strategies. Below are some examples class participants have shared over the years about ending an interaction:

I practiced on the bus. When someone sat next to me and started talking, I said, "You know, I don't really want to have a conversation right now." Then I turned and looked out the window.

At a party someone cornered me in the kitchen. I felt trapped. I was literally in the corner. Finally, I put my hand on her shoulder and said, "I am going to go get a drink" and walked away. I was nervous, I felt guilty that she would be hurt but I also felt good about it.

I have a friendship that has become toxic in the past few years. I really love him. We have been friends since we were in grade school running around the neighborhood. We did everything together all through high school. It is hard for me to think about not being friends. But I had to end it. I didn't do it in a way I am proud of. I slowly stopped sending him messages, kind of cutting him out bit by bit. I think he figured out what I was doing because he stopped texting me and we just kind of drifted apart. I miss him, but it just wasn't working.

I told my mother I couldn't talk to her for a while. I told her that it was just too hard on me emotionally and that I would get in touch with her when I was ready. She was upset and I don't think she really got why I needed space, which is part of the whole reason I need it [in the first place].

My girlfriend is a talker and after a long day sometimes it's too much. I used to try to tell her this but we would end up talking about that, which didn't help. After taking this class, I tried putting my hand on her leg, smiling, and just said, "I love you, I can't talk right now." Then sat there next to her holding her hand.

It's hard at work. I am a cashier and sometimes people just start telling you things. Last week when a lady started talking about her daughter and I knew she would be there forever, I smiled a big smile and said, "I am sorry, I hate to interrupt you, but I really need to get back to work."

This man approached me at the bus stop starting to ask me my name and where I was going and I put my hand up, palm facing him, and shook my head no. He looked surprised. I shifted so I wasn't facing him and ignored him.

I broke off a relationship after things started getting bad. It took a while. I wanted to try to make it work and I know I stayed longer than I should have because I knew that he acted the way he did because of the things he had gone through when he was a kid. At some point though, it just didn't matter. I left. I wrote a letter and left while he was at work.

I use humor a lot. As a bartender you get used to setting limits with people, you have to. When someone is pushy or not listening I will joke with them and if that doesn't work, I let them know that if they don't listen to me they will be asked to leave, no discussion. I let them know it's up to them—they can listen to me or get kicked out. It is their choice.

I just walked away. It felt weird but also really cool. This guy at work talks nonstop. When you go to the break room he will follow you and start talking. I used to try to wait for a break and then say something about having to get back to work but it was hard because he would just follow me back to my desk and keep talking. This time I grabbed my coffee, smiled, turned my back on him, and walked back to my desk.

Terminating a conversation, relationship, or leaving an event or situation will be challenging for different people in different ways and in various contexts. Believing that it is acceptable to walk away, halt, interrupt, stop, redirect, and ultimately END AN INTERACTION is critical to boundary setting and boundary health. From quitting a toxic employment situation, disentangling oneself from an unhealthy relationship, ending an offensive conversation, interrupting an unsafe scenario, or getting out of a dangerous situation, ending an interaction is an important skill.

WRAPPING IT UP

NAME THE BEHAVIOR, GIVE A DIRECTIVE, BROKEN RECORD, and END AN INTERACTION are not the only ways to set and negotiate boundaries. They are a few basic tools to get you started or to add to your interpersonal repertoire. The intent of these skills is to support boundary setting that helps people negotiate, explore, communicate, and when necessary, defend wants, needs, and limits.

The goal of integrating these skills into our lives and relationships is to increase our capacity to navigate the complications of interpersonal interactions in a more grounded way. The next chapter examines challenges to using these skills and provides suggestions and examples for handling them.

THREE

CHALLENGES AND DOUBTS

WE SET BOUNDARIES WITH ALL KINDS OF PEOPLE IN A VARIETY OF different situations. Some will be easy to navigate while others may involve serious challenges and obstacles. Everyone is different and what feels overwhelming to one person will be a nonissue to someone else. Sometimes setting boundaries feels natural or instinctive. Other times it might seem counterintuitive or impossible to set a boundary. One person may find it easy to name the behavior with strangers, while someone else feels more comfortable using GIVE A DIRECTIVE with friends. For some people, setting boundaries with their family brings up intense anxiety. For others, saying no to anyone in a role of authority seems nearly impossible. Particular situations will require different types of boundaries and how boundaries are identified and communicated will be informed by people's skills, capacity, and experience. This chapter considers how to identify and navigate difficult or challenging situations, how to learn from mistakes, and offers some ideas on dealing with doubts and insecurities.

CHALLENGES AS GROWTH

Rather than judge ourselves (or others) for the things we find difficult or are unskilled at, we can be aware of the things which challenge us and use them to help us grow. It's not bad to feel unskilled at asking a partner for more physical touch. And it's not good if someone else is confident in asking for more touch. It's simply a difference in comfort, experience, skill level, personality, cultural values, norms, or individuality. It is helpful to know what contexts are difficult to set boundaries in, what skills need to be learned or practiced, and when might be a good time for support or guidance. As discussed in chapter two, in addition to identifying wants and needs, it is helpful to be aware of various elements that comprise the context in which boundaries are being set, including barriers, challenges, concerns, and emotional hooks. The more we know about ourselves the better we will be able to set, maintain, or negotiate boundaries across a variety of different situations.

In teaching boundary-setting classes, I noticed that some participants believed that their boundary needed to be explained, justified, or defended. That is, if the other person did not understand and/or agree with a boundary, they often worried that it was not justified or reasonable. This belief puts a lot of pressure on a person to be able to explain or rationalize a boundary, something that is not always possible or even desirable. While most class participants claimed they had a right to set a boundary that someone didn't like or agree with, it became apparent that when faced with this situation (during class role plays and exercises), many people did not know how to handle it, especially when navigating boundaries in scenarios that involved people they knew and wanted to maintain some kind of a relationship with. The conviction that everyone has a right to set boundaries that may upset or offend people was challenging for some students to put into "real time" practice. They struggled to justify and got hooked into explaining their boundary, often leaving them feeling confused, upset, and overwhelmed. It became clear that an important part of mastering boundary-setting skills was learning how to set a boundary without explaining or justifying it. It also became evident that an important auxiliary skill set was to help people identify and address thoughts, emotions, and interpretations that arise in response to people's reactions (or anticipated reactions) to a boundary.

Excuses or justifications are sometimes used to avoid the emotional content (guilt, fear, shame, anxiety …) of setting a boundary. Justifications dislocate the boundary as separate from, and outside the responsibility of, the person setting it. "I won't" or "I don't want to" instead becomes "I can't." This tactic is not good or bad, but it is important to know when it may be helpful to defend, explain, or justify a boundary, and when it might not be desirable or necessary. Sometimes it is essential that the person understand (and agree with) a boundary. A mother in a boundary-setting workshop shares an example:

> I needed to ask my boss to let me off early or at least right on time. My daughter's daycare had started to charge for a full hour even if you were just a minute late. I couldn't afford to be late at all. My boss asks everyone to stay late sometimes, so that was a situation where it felt really important to justify my boundary with her and not just say, "I can't stay late" or "I am leaving right when my shift ends" without explaining why.

Problems arise when the boundary setter believes they can't set or maintain a boundary when someone does not understand or agree with it. Another woman in a self-defense class shares an example of being in such a situation:

> I really wanted my sister to understand that I couldn't talk to our aunt anymore. I needed to set this boundary. My aunt had been really abusive to her son growing up and is mean to my sister and me when we see her. At some point I realized I was an adult and didn't have to take it. My sister didn't understand. In her mind, it was all in the past and none of it was a big deal. I tried to explain it to her but she just didn't get it. I ended up giving in because I didn't want this to come between my sister and me. She is the closest family I have and it didn't seem worth it at that point for me to push it. I didn't like it, but at that time I didn't know what else to do. I didn't really feel like I could set that boundary unless she was on board.

Sometimes the process of explaining a boundary can help people become more certain about it. Other times, it can feel as if you are slowly being talked out of your boundary, or doubts begin to creep in. Doubts are powerful. Doubts (ours or someone else's) can drain and divert attention and energy away from setting a boundary toward defending or justifying it. At times, explaining or rationalizing a boundary leads people so far astray that the boundary itself gets lost. A class participant's story illustrates such a scenario:

> I was young and hanging out with this boy. He wanted to go further than I did sexually. I remember saying something like I didn't think it was a good idea and he had all these reasons why it was okay. I told him I didn't want to get in trouble and he had all these ways of making sure we wouldn't. After a while, I just got tired. And a little confused. I wanted to do some things with him but not everything he wanted. The more we talked, the more confused I felt. He had an answer for every concern I put out there. It was overwhelming and I ended up doing some things I didn't really want to.

DEALING WITH DOUBTS

There are a few ways we can handle doubts: cheerlead, challenge, ignore, or listen. Each approach is helpful at different times. When we cheer ourselves, we give ourselves support and encouragement: *You can do it!* This may involve encouraging ourselves or asking for support and cheerleading from friends, family, or other support systems. The cheerleading may address specific skills, talents, or personal qualities: *I am creative. You are loved. I am a compassionate person. I am an important part of my work team.* Or be more general: *You rock! I am fabulous. I can get through this. You deserve this.* Sometimes cheerleading is like a team of supporters yelling loudly, "You can do it!" Other times, cheerleading is quieter, softer, soothing: *It is going to be okay.* It is important to find statements that resonate and fit with what is desired, given the context. Some examples could include: *You are smart. Learning (a new skill) is difficult. It's okay to feel scared. Everyone makes mistakes. You are loved. It is not the end of the world. You are tenacious. I am worthy of love. It's okay for me to ask for what I want.* Cheerleading can also be physical and nonverbal. Letting a friend or loved one comfort you when you cry, a hug, an arm squeeze, a wink, a smile, a back rub, can all be forms of cheerleading. There are a myriad of ways to communicate support and encouragement.

Challenging doubts involves countering myths and untruths we tell about ourselves, others, or situations. It also includes identifying and interrupting catastrophizing thoughts.[5] This means being able to both recognize myths, untruths, or catastrophizing thoughts and offer clear, direct statements that refute them. It is not always easy to identify the myths and untruths we have come to believe, as one workshop participant points out:

It's hard to tell reality from the voices that shaped your world growing up. It feels crazy at first to think that it is possible to have a different way of seeing things, of seeing yourself. But if you can tolerate the crazy feeling, you feel liberated, like you can really be yourself and see the world through your own eyes. Growing up, I was told I was stupid in really direct and indirect ways. I still carry that view of myself. But I have been learning that it is okay to make mistakes, to mess up, or even to just be human and not know things and that doesn't make me stupid. I am beginning to understand that other people don't see me that way and that makes it possible for me to see myself in a new way. Like, maybe I am not stupid even when I feel really stupid. That feeling comes from an old place, not from what is happening in the moment.

Recognizing catastrophizing thoughts is a helpful skill. While it can be helpful to imagine possible pitfalls or negative outcomes, catastrophizing is not planning. Planning or strategizing is recognizing a variety of possible outcomes, including desirable and non-desirable results. Catastrophizing is focusing only on the negative possibilities.

---

[5]   To "catastrophize" something means to focus on the negative and worst possible aspects of a current situation, or the outcome of a future or past event. When someone catastrophizes something, they are unable to see or imagine any positive possibilities, as if everything is/ was/will be a catastrophe. Think Eeyore from *Winnie the Pooh.*

When I thought about getting a new job, I only thought of all the bad things that could happen. When I wanted to move, all I could think of was how much worse it could be. I couldn't see how it could be better. Even though I was not happy, I stopped myself every time I tried to move in a direction to make myself happy. I got in my own way. I had a negative loop going on at all times. It was draining and made hope impossible. Once I recognized this as catastrophizing, I was able to see it for what it was—a negative pattern—and began to imagine that things could work out for me in a positive way. When bad things happened, they no longer proved that things would never work out.

—CLASS PARTICIPANT

MYTHS, CHALLENGES, AND CHEERLEADING STATEMENTS

Recognizing catastrophizing thoughts allows them to be named for what they are: thoughts. Challenge statements name and interrupt worry and catastrophizing thoughts, and counter myths or untruths. Below are some examples that class participants have come up with:

MYTH	CHALLENGE STATEMENT
I am stupid.	Not everyone knows everything all the time.
I can't change jobs, no one will hire me.	It may be difficult, but you've faced difficult times before.
Everyone at school hates me.	There may be people who don't like you, but there are other people who do like and love you.
I am a horrible person.	What you did was not okay, but you are not a horrible person.
I yelled at my partner and called her names.	Doing something bad does not make you a bad person.

Cheerleading and challenge statements can overlap at times. *It's okay to be a beginner. Mistakes don't mean you are stupid. Everyone gets rejected at some point. Just because someone was mean to you doesn't mean you did anything wrong. We all hurt people's feelings at times, it's not the end of the world. So you embarrassed yourself at the party, everyone has regrettable moments in their lives.* These are all examples of statements that counter a myth and offer encouragement. Being able to identify what would be helpful for you in a given situation means that you can ask for what you want and need. Maybe encouragement falls flat and that is a sign that the myth still looms large and it will be more helpful to focus on countering it. Other times, what we want is to know we have a cheerleading squad rooting for us. Boundary work is about identifying and asking for wants and needs to be met.

You can also use the BROKEN RECORD strategy that was discussed in the previous chapter by repeating the cheerleading or challenge statement over and over. Being a broken record creates a barrier between you and your doubts and helps redirect and keep attention on the boundary. It allows you to acknowledge the presence of doubt, or other feelings and thoughts, and not get caught up in them. To some degree, cheerleading and challenging keeps one engaged with doubts. While this is not bad, it is helpful to know when and how to disengage. Like an insistent three-year-old in a grocery store who wants a candy bar, doubts can keep going and going until they wear you down. Sometimes doubts keep poking holes in challenge or cheerleading statements until they find a myth or untruth that you don't have a challenge or cheerleading statement about. When this happens, it is easy to feel overwhelmed with doubt or believe the lack of cheerleading or challenge statements proves the doubt to be true. In reality, all this proves is that, at this time, you do not have a counter or cheerleading statement. In other words, cheerleading and challenging can be helpful but they can also backfire. Having the skill to ignore or, at times, listen to doubts is important.

DIRECTING ATTENTION ELSEWHERE

Another way to handle doubts is to recognize them, then ignore them altogether. You acknowledge doubts as what they are: doubts. Then you direct your attention elsewhere. You choose to turn your attention, your mind, toward what you want to focus on and away from doubts and catastrophizing thoughts. This can be very challenging. Doubts are powerful. The first step in ignoring them is realizing that they have taken our attention or consumed the mind. It is impossible to redirect our attention until we are aware that doubts have taken over. Think about a time when you were worried about something and it was difficult to think of anything else. Worrying thoughts cycle through the mind over and over—spinning mental wheels, as they are often described. First, recognize the worrying thoughts, then name them for what they are: doubts or thoughts. Then direct your attention to something else. Sometimes this process has to be repeated many times in a single minute. While this may feel frustrating or maddening at first, like building up muscle, it gets stronger the more you use it. A client shares his thoughts about naming and disengaging from doubts:

> When I first practiced naming doubts then trying to ignore them, it felt impossible. I could think about something else for maybe a second, then I would be right back in my doubts and shame. Over time, though, I noticed I could turn my mind more and more and I was doing it without having to totally concentrate. Now, I feel a lot stronger in being able to recognize when I am in that thought cycle and disengage from it. It's not always easy but it's getting easier.

It is important to be aware that doubts will return over and over to demand our attention and that ignoring them can be very difficult. A client of mine compared disregarding doubts to trying to ignore a giant screaming monster running around in your head. We explored how the more he learned to ignore this monster, challenging as it was, the less power it had over him, and how it got smaller and quieter over time.

BEFRIENDING YOUR INNER DEMON

There is an exercise a yoga teacher shared with me many years ago called "Befriending Your Inner Demon." Befriending your inner demon is turning toward intense and distressing thoughts, emotions, sensations, images, or memories with a sense of patience, loving kindness, and openness, and then asking what the thought/sensation/image monster (or "demon") needs. In this case, we are practicing turning toward doubts and asking them what they want or need. The quality of the question is not demanding or threatening. Think of a crying infant. Your job, when faced with a crying baby, is to figure out what the cry means. Is it a hungry cry? Sleepy cry? Full-diaper cry? Want to be sung to cry? Of course, our inner demons are not infants and like the monster mentioned above, they can be frightening and imposing. But if we turn toward them with the same quality of compassionate curiosity, we are more likely to find out what the need is, where the doubt comes from, and what will help quiet it. A client shares her experience:

> I was so scared to face my negative voices and all the doubts that told me I was nothing, that I was full of shame because I was a horrible person. I know these feelings have to do with what happened when I was a kid, but that doesn't change them. When I started turning to face the voices and the darkness, I felt small and powerless but then I kept asking, "What do you need?" At one point, I said out loud, "You keep showing up every time I try to make a decision that will make me happy, telling me I don't deserve it, so clearly you need something. What is it that you want or need?" Turns out, it sounds so hokey, but it was the pain I felt as a little girl. She was hurt and pissed and scared because no one kept her safe and she ended up feeling like it was her fault. She needed me to tell her it wasn't her fault, and I needed her to be okay with me deserving things.

It is critical that the naming and asking be done as compassionately and neutrally as possible, using factual, nonjudgmental language that is free from story telling or meaning-making. Turning toward our inner demon with self-loathing and judgment tends to discourage the discovery of (and tending to) wants and needs, and rather tends to provoke defensiveness and a closing off. A client shares:

When I felt jealous, I used to judge myself really harshly. I have strong values about unconditional love and not being possessive. Whenever I felt jealous, it felt like I was not enacting my values. I would get really down on myself. I understood that jealously was a product of how we view relationships and I thought that at some point, if I worked hard enough, I would evolve to not feeling jealous. It took a long time to understand that jealously was a feeling, not an action or behavior that I could control. When I stopped trying to not feel jealous and stopped beating myself up for feeling jealous, it was a lot easier to deal with the feeling. I could name it, be kind to myself, discover what I needed in that moment, and then move on.

Beating ourselves up for feeling doubt or judging ourselves for "worry thoughts" only adds distress to the doubts and worry. The practice of identifying and reframing judgments or meaning-making statements is an important part of boundary work.

WHEN AND HOW TO LISTEN TO DOUBTS

Finally, there may be times when you want to listen to doubt and let it inform your decisions and actions. Doubt may, at times, provide information about a real concern. In classes, people have asked how to tell the difference between a doubt manufactured by insecurity, shame, guilt, or stories we tell ourselves based on experiences and "real" doubts or doubts rooted in our inner self and authentic experience. There is not a formula or cheat sheet to distinguish between these, but many people have described the experience of feeling real or true doubt as different from experiencing doubt that comes from a lack of self-trust, insecurity, shame, self-consciousness, or feelings of unworthiness. It is worth taking some time to notice the total experience (feelings, thoughts, body sensations) of different doubts and learn to recognize when you want to listen to them, when you want to acknowledge and ignore them, and when you want to cheerlead or use counter statements. A client talks about their experience with identifying doubts:

The more I practiced identifying what I wanted in a situation, the more I was able to tell when the doubts or negative thoughts were really my inner voice and when they were coming from the other voice, the one that finds so many ways to tell me I am silly or stupid or selfish. When that voice comes up, I feel a tightening in my chest and get short of breath. I am learning to be aware of those sensations and not react to them but listen to them. When the doubt is my inner voice, me, it feels different, like it is really coming from inside me, my center near my forehead and also in my gut. It's hard to explain, but it is a different thing altogether.

Doubts, like making mistakes and grappling with challenges, are a fundamental part of life, relationships, and boundary setting. Learning how to skillfully handle incertitude is essential to boundary setting. Having options and being able to intentionally ignore, challenge, or listen to doubts reduces the power they have to derail, drain, and distract while giving people more agency and capacity in negotiating wants and needs.

FOUR

INTUITION AND THE REFLECTIVE LOOP

IN CHAPTER TWO WE COVERED SEVERAL TOOLS: NAME THE BEHAVIOR, GIVE A DIRECTIVE, BROKEN RECORD, and END AN INTERACTION. These tools are *what* we do: identify a behavior, express what we want someone to do, repeat our boundary or directive, and end an interaction. Now we will explore *how* to do these skills. First, I introduce ideas about how to use intuition and self-reflection to set boundaries. Then I will explore some ways that intuition and boundaries are socially constructed. Intuition is an important tool that has the power to guide decisions but can also reinforce stereotypes. This chapter takes a look at intuition and offers tips on how to tap into intuition with an understanding of the ways in which it may be influenced by social constructs. This chapter also offers tools for recognizing and responding to fears and challenges involved in boundary setting, including ways to engage in reality checks, accountability, and self-reflective skills.

INTUITION

Different people describe and view intuition in various ways. In an online interview, author Thomas Condon writes, "Intuition is a lot like dreaming. We don't know how we do it, but we do it. Intuition is knowing something, but not knowing how you know it. Intuitive knowledge comes to us spontaneously and directly, without the use of reason or logical thought …"[6] Scientists often view intuition in a different light, seeing it as a biological reaction to stimuli, similar to the flight or fight response. Marsha Linehan, founder of Dialectical Behavioral Therapy, compares intuition to what she calls Wise Mind, a mind in balance between emotion and rational logic. In classes, participants have compared intuition to their gut, a sense or knowing, a sixth sense, a belief that we get talked out of, inner self, deep self, the voice inside your head/heart/gut/soul, true voice, or the person under all the social static or noise. A class participant shares their ideas about intuition:

> *Intuition is this sense you have. It's like you know something that you may not know you know. Which is why I think it is so easy to get talked out of trusting it. It may not make sense. Like you get a weird or off feeling, but there isn't any "evidence" to justify your feeling so you ignore it. I think we have to learn to trust it even if we can't "prove" it.*

I believe intuition is all of these things and involves three basic components: sensing, knowing, and feeling. Someone might sense that they are being followed as they are walking home and become scared. The sensation that signals fear (tingling in the head, a knot in the stomach, or heat in the face—it's different for everyone) is prescribed meaning because of the context and story we tell about the situation. In the above example, the context is walking home and the sensations signal danger and the subsequent feeling, fear.

While the awareness of being followed may be inherent or biological, the meaning is socially constructed. In a different context, say walking through a crowded campus, the same sensations created by the awareness of being followed might be interpreted as excitement because the person is expecting their friend to meet them. In both

---

6   www.awakening-intuition.com

cases, the sensations triggered by becoming aware of being followed are the same (tingling in the head, an impulse to turn around), but the interpretation is different, thus so is the subsequent feeling. Sensations located on or in the body are what we typically identify as intuition, but they are only one part. Perception is the meaning we ascribe to a sensation and what guides and prompts us toward action. Perception is the meaning assigned to a situation or interaction, and is based on context, social constructs, and personal experiences. In other words, people are taught how to interpret sensations through social learning.

Personal space is a good example. Personal space is a social construct. Different cultures have different ideas of what personal space is. Even the term "personal space" is Western, locating the self at the center of a particular social space. When someone says they felt like their personal space was invaded and it made them feel unsafe, they are typically referring to sensing, knowing, and feeling. There is the biological response of the sensations that signal their personal space has been invaded (tingling on their skin, tightening stomach muscles, a reflexive pulling back), the interpretation of these sensations based on social learning and personal experience, and then finally the feeling associated with the interpretation—in this case, feeling fearful or unsafe.

In the United States, we culturally expect much more personal space than in many other countries. Growing up in the United Sates, one is exposed to all kinds of messages about physical, social, environmental, personal and interpersonal space. While there are differences among subcultures, the overall mainstream norms are formed through socialization, social systems, structures, and even architecture. We absorb norms about space that feel "natural," often not even noticing it until we are exposed to different norms. In other cultures, however, someone standing close by would not trigger the same biological or physiological responses.

Finally, perceptions are also shaped by personal experience. If someone grows up in a physically demonstrative family with cultural messages about personal space and touch that value physical close-ness, they may have very different boundaries around being touched than someone who grew up with messages that physical closeness is a private matter. Individual experience also comes into play. If someone is very comfortable with close, personal space but has been sexually harassed by a coworker, boundaries around hugging acquaintances may change. Biological and physiological responses, sensations, and perceptions of what it means to be hugged by a coworker, informed by social learning, are also impacted by personal experience.

SOCIAL CONDITIONING AFFECTS INTUITION

A sensation triggers a biological/physical/automatic response in our bodies. We interpret or know the sensation based on personal experience and social learning. This is the thinking or knowing part of intuition. Both of these help identify feelings and the feeling helps us decide how we want to respond. Sensations, while located primarily in the body, are also affected by social conditioning. We are taught how we should perceive things.

If people trust their intuition without being aware of how it has been socially constructed, they risk using it in ways that uphold stereotypes, misinformation, and systems of oppression. In my experience, it is fairly common in self-defense and boundary-setting classes for participants to ask, "What do you do if a stranger approaches you?" This question often arises during discussions about trusting one's intuition. In classes, people have stated that they are learning to trust their intuition and that it kicks in when a stranger approaches them on the street. Class participants who are exploring which boundary-setting or self-defense skills to use may feel extra sensitive to this scenario, wondering, *is it better to stand one's ground or walk away quickly?* I tell them there is no single answer. Intuition must be tempered with an understanding of how social constructs and personal assumptions affect us.

It's easy to suggest to class participants that they feel empowered enough to trust their instincts and respond accordingly. This may involve walking away, not making eye contact, setting a boundary, or using body language to effectively communicate their boundary. Yet understanding how social constructs inform intuition requires us to explore a bit more before simply trusting our intuition. In the scenario above where people are asking how to respond to a stranger approaching them on the street, it would be helpful to investigate what their intuition is telling them. Is it telling them that this stranger is dangerous? That they should be afraid of this person? What is the fear based on? Is it only because the person is a stranger? What is the stranger doing that signals danger? Anything? Are people afraid because of what the person looks like?

Many class participants have shared a fear of men who appear homeless and approach them on the street and often ask for spare change. When questions about how to respond in these types of situations arise, I encourage people to imagine what the person is doing and what they imagine the person looks like. Are you afraid because the person is a large, unshaven man with a dirty jacket? Is it because he is muttering or shouting? Or appears to be drunk and carrying a bottle that could be used as a weapon? Is it because he is walking toward you? If so, what is it about how the person is walking toward you that signals danger? Would you have the same psychological and biological sensations, and subsequently the same feelings, and ascribe the same meaning to the feeling if someone in a business suit walked toward you in the same way? Why or why not? Would you have the same intuitive response if a young girl approached you in a similar context? Is the person doing anything that you can identify as signaling a threat? If not, one should wonder whether intuition in this case might be based on a stereotype that strangers in general, and people who are perceived as homeless in particular, are viewed as dangerous.

It is worth considering how the discomfort someone feels from an approaching stranger whom they perceive as homeless can also be a reflection of the dehumanizing social messages about homelessness and people struggling with housing rather than an actual danger. The social constructs that stereotype homeless people as dangerous or threatening ignore the reality of violence against homeless people, people who are much more likely to be victims than perpetrators. "Cities often focus on cracking down on panhandling or sleeping outside as a way to push homeless people out of sight," says National Law Center on Homelessness and Poverty (NLCH) Civil Rights Program Director Tulin Ozdeger. "The numbers show the need for a different response—training police to help protect homeless people and deliver needed services, not to lock them up in jail."

In order for intuition to be an effective boundary-setting tool, it is important to consider "gut feelings" as well as evidence, facts, and factors of social conditioning. If we are taught through media and social constructs to be afraid of people, particularly men who appear homeless, we might experience an "intuitive" sense of fear when passing a male who is panhandling on the street, even if all he's doing is holding out a cup and calling out to us. We need to ask ourselves whether our fear is truly our intuition or is it born from social conditioning? This approach asks people to not blindly trust intuition, but to really get to know it—make sure intuitiveness is grounded in emotional experience, as well as what is actually happening. Is the man doing something other than simply panhandling that makes you feel fear?

The media and social constructs also send the message to fear black people in general, and black men in particular; this socially constructed fear has now become ingrained as Jennifer Eberhardt and her colleagues suggest:

Simply thinking of crime can lead perceivers to conjure up images of Black Americans that "ready" these perceivers to register and selectively attend to Black people ... these associations are important not only because they can lead perceivers to make mistakes occasionally but also because they can guide, generally, how perceivers come to organize and structure visual stimuli to which they are exposed.[7]

---

[7] Eberhardt, Jennifer E., Phillip A. Goff, Valerie J. Purdie, and Paul G. Davies. "Seeing Black: Race, Crime, and Visual Processing." *Journal of Personality and Social Psychology*. Vol 87(6), Dec 2004: 876-93.

In other words, the link between African Americans and crime has become so thoroughly conditioned that these associations occur regardless of individual values or beliefs about crime, violence, or racial disparity. This is not intuition. This is an example of how fears are, in part, socially constructed.

Intuition is important. It is critical that people learn to listen to and trust their intuition, but it is vital that this is done mindfully. There are all sorts of factors that prevent people from trusting their intuition and learning to "trust our gut" is an essential skill. It is important that this skill be developed with an understanding of how all sorts of things, including racism, homophobia, classism, oppressive systems of gender, ableism, and ageism inform intuition. Intuition is a gift. It is important to nurture, listen to, and seriously dialogue with it because it can often be misconstrued or misinterpreted.

THE INTUITION MYTH OF PREVENTION

In classes, I have witnessed the false belief that if someone is tuned into their intuition, they can prevent something bad from happening. This belief is understandable. Fear of awful, unfortunate, and horrible events drives people to seek clear and prescriptive ways to prevent them. Unfortunately, the belief that having heightened intuition can help prevent bad things from happening not only puts judgment and blame on survivors (*I should have seen this coming*), it perpetuates the falsehood that intuition is the key to prevention. Intuition can be proactive and preventative, but not always. It can kick in as a response to something, or upon self-reflection, surface after an event. Intuition is not a superhero's skill or a sixth sense. It is a practical tool that one can master. Like any tool, mastery takes time, it takes practice, and it involves making mistakes. The REFLEC-TIVE LOOP helps us explore and deepen the capacity to critically listen to and use our intuition.

THE REFLECTIVE LOOP

The REFLECTIVE LOOP is a mechanism used to explore intuition and boundaries. The loop involves the flow of communication or reflection between you, your support systems, the boundary itself, and the people you are setting the boundary with. As implied by the name, the loop is circular in that you can begin a check-in or reflective process at any point on the loop. The loop is also a holon, meaning the parts, while separate, also inform one another and comprise a whole. A holon is a system or entity (in this case a reflective system) that is simultaneously a whole and a part. Arthur Koestler coined the term holon in his book *The Ghost in the Machine* and author Michael Pollan more recently popularized the concept in his book *An Omnivore's Dilemma.* Koestler defines a holon as a hierarchy of self-regulating, dependent, and interdependent parts that function in coordination with their local environment. In other words, there is no specific point from which to start, or a precise way to distinguish between or measure the cause and effect. In the case of the REFLECTIVE LOOP, feedback and reflection inform the actions that change feedback systems, which inform relationships and boundaries in a myriad of multifaceted, and sometimes simultaneously and seemingly oppositional, ways.

When using the REFLECTIVE LOOP, it is important that communication and contemplation on and between each aspect of the loop be nonjudgmental, non-shaming, honest, and connected to your values. The loop offers a way to get feedback and "reality checks" about your boundaries. Reality checks are a means to hold yourself accountable to your values and a way of being accountable for both the boundaries you set and how you set them. You may check in with your support system before, during, or after setting a boundary to explore a variety of aspects, including the motivation for setting it, the effect and impact of setting it, desired outcome or goal of the boundary, your emotional response, safety needs, and social and cultural considerations. Reality checks challenge people to explore events, situations, and interactions in non-shaming ways and encourage creative problem-solving that is rooted in radical acceptance, commitment to values, and personal wants and needs. A class participant shares an example:

> My husband and I had just moved, and my mom came to visit her sister who lives nearby and was in the hospital. It was assumed my mom would stay with us. I didn't want her to stay with us and I felt really guilty about it. My mom is pretty dependent on extended family members to help her with things; she can't drive or get around on the bus and things like that. I was trying to figure out what to do. I talked to my friends, my husband, my sister, and then finally to my mom to figure out what might happen depending on different decisions I made—it was important to consider the impact, not only on my mom and other family members (which is what I have always done), but also on me and my husband. I had to learn to sit with the guilt and not react out of it. I ended up deciding to have her stay with us, but it felt good to go through the loop to help me so that I didn't just make that decision out of guilt.

People can use the REFLECTIVE LOOP system to identify and then get support for emotions that arise. Intense or distressing feelings may make people doubt their intuition or question their right to set a boundary. Sometimes people become defensive and angry or guilty and ashamed at prioritizing needs or setting a new kind of boundary. Or, people may be proud of setting a new kind of boundary and want acknowledgment. The REFLECTIVE LOOP can be used to explore ways to renegotiate a boundary, to consider how to respond to emotions that arise, or to maintain a challenging boundary. Some questions to consider when using the REFLECTIVE LOOP could include the following: Are you setting the boundary from a place of emotional integrity? Is the boundary consistent with your values? If not, why not? Is there anything you can do or want to do to make the boundary more in line with your values? What feelings, thoughts, and sensations arise when you think about setting or actually set the boundary? Are there particular reactions that bring up intense emotions for you? Are there any reasons you would want to change or renegotiate the boundary? Are there any conditions in which you would choose to not set the boundary? What impact do you anticipate the boundary having on you and/or the person/people you are setting the boundary with?

CHECKING INTUITION

The loop can help ground boundaries in a critical and thoughtful framework. Following up on the earlier example, intuition may tell us that a man who appears homeless or who is panhandling and approaches us is dangerous. We may choose to act on our intuition by telling him to get away from us when he approaches us. We can then use the self-reflective loop to do a reality check and use our support systems to get feedback. Was my intuition based on stereotypes or real evidence that I needed to set a boundary? Was the man's behavior truly aggressive, or was my perception of danger informed by fear-based prejudices? It is important to explore these aspects of boundaries in an honest and non-judging, non-shaming way. Judging and shaming are not helpful tools for reflection and personal growth.

Reflecting on our past actions may also allow us to formulate a plan for dealing with events in the future. Using the previous example, we may decide upon reflection that in a similar situation (a stranger approaching us on the street), if we perceive any aggressive behavior (loud voice, drunkenness, a possible weapon, etc.), we will quickly turn around and walk away. However, if we perceive no aggressive action, we might decide to practice looking the person in the eye, acknowledging their humanity, and be prepared to greet them and see what they asking for.

BEING AWARE OF JUDGMENT

Exploring and reflecting on choices, behaviors, and motivations in a nonjudgmental way can be challenging. Like any new skill (riding a bike, mastering a computer program, speaking a second language, practicing yoga, joining a hockey team, taking horseback riding lessons, surfing, writing a poem, organizing a benefit show, playing an instrument, writing music, cooking a new kind of fabulous meal, saving money, etc.), it takes patience, practice, and making a lot of mistakes. In the beginning it can be helpful to practice being aware of judgment. Learning to recognize a judgment takes time, as it often feels like truth or reality. After cultivating an awareness of judgment, it can be helpful to practice reframing judgment or shaming self-talk into nonjudgmental and non-shaming talk. This can feel awkward at first, but it gets easier. A client shares an example:

> *When I started becoming aware of how much I judge myself, I judged myself for judging myself! It was really hard to stop. I never realized how often I was super hard on myself. I'd call myself stupid or other names without even realizing it. After I got used to recognizing judgments, I started reframing them. I'd be able to be kinder to myself, more like I would be if someone else came to me with the same situation. I would never call them stupid or think they are an idiot. At first it felt like I was letting myself off the hook, like if I stopped judging myself I would never change or move forward. But the more compassionate I was, the more I could imagine how things could be different and how I could take steps toward that.*

After a friend of mine quit smoking, she would still "blow it" and smoke. As we talked about what was going on and how she could integrate a nonjudgmental framework into quitting, she realized something important. When she would blow it, she would feel ashamed and say and feel horrible things about herself (*I'm such a loser, I'm weak, I'll never be able to do this*), which would make her feel even worse. This made it difficult to explore what was going on before, during, or after the times she "blew it." She didn't want to explore these incidents because it was so shaming and when she tried, she ran right into her jumble of judgments. When we reframed these "blow it" moments from moments of exploration into what actually triggered an urge she felt she couldn't resist, she began to have more self-awareness, which made it easier to anticipate these situations, prepare for them, and when possible, prevent them.

It's important to reiterate that non-judgment is not the same as reframing a negative into a positive. Saying a person is nice, lovely, or a great friend is a judgment—the same as if one labels a person as mean, miserable, or an awful friend. What a nonjudgmental framework does is ask people to describe something using facts or descriptions rather than using judgments as shorthand. Judgments are easy shorthand. An example might be, "Julie remembers our conversations and this makes me feel like she listens to me and is interested in what I have to say." This is a statement using descriptive facts. "Julie is nice" is a judgment. It is also a much shorter, briefer statement. Nonjudgmental reframing typically takes more time, more words, and more description, which can feel cumbersome in some situations. The goal is not to avoid shorthand or describe someone as nice. The goal is to become aware of using shorthand, to be intentional when choosing to use it, and to be able to reframe statements when helpful. Practicing nonjudgmental frameworks does not imply that judgments are bad (a judgment of judgment!) nor that people should never make or use judgments. Judgments are useful in assessing risks, sizing up a situation or interaction, and providing helpful shorthand. Rather, this skill is about being able to recognize when judgments are being used in ways that are not helpful and then being able to reframe in nonjudgmental way. This process can offer different perspectives. Another client shares an example:

> When I am able to use nonjudgmental language with myself and other people, it opens up so much space. I find that there are options, choices that I never felt were possible. My parents are really conservative and I am not. I used to judge them and felt judged by them whenever we spent any time together. I thought I should somehow either be impenetrable and never let them and their conservative ideology get to me, or that I could

magically change them. When I stopped judging myself, our relationship changed. I actually stopped judging them, too. I didn't stop calling them out or sharing my opinion or defending myself, but now it feels calmer, like I am coming from a different, less defensive place.

REFLECTION AND REALITY CHECKS

Reality checks and support systems can give us information about emotional or psychological hooks. In this context, when people get "hooked" it means that the hook itself (or the attempt to avoid it) is in some way driving behaviors, decisions, and actions. For example, someone may not want to feel a particular emotion and the desire to not feel it drives their decisions to the detriment of themselves or their relationships. It could mean that a feeling is so strong and over-whelming that it becomes the primary lens through which decisions are made. In other words, when someone gets hooked, whatever the hook may be (guilt, shame, indecision, anxiety, avoidance, fear of con-flict), it is the principle force behind behaviors. Sometimes people are conscious of their hooks, other times they are not. The REFLECTIVE LOOP helps people be more attuned when hooks are happening and find ways to address this.

Reality checks and support systems work together. Support systems provide emotional, spiritual, mental, and physical care. When done in non-shaming and non-judging ways, this kind of support strengthens the capacity of reality checks. Reality checks offer a critical look at, and constructive criticism and feedback about, events, interactions, and boundaries. When done well, reality checks take into account individual personalities and experiences, as well as social, environ-mental, cultural, political, and other contextual information. Having outside reflection, and learning to reflect back to ourselves in a non-shaming way is important. To some degree, reality checks are similar to learning to attend to the quality of the air around us. Most of us don't really pay much attention to air unless it is particularly bad (or good), but tuning into the quality of air that we live in offers a wealth of information, including how we may need and want to attend to it. The relationship between supports and reality checks is an important part of the REFLECTIVE LOOP. The more we tune into and tend to them, the stronger and more vibrant they become. The stronger our supports and reality checks are, the more we will be able to set and negotiate boundaries that reflect our wants and needs in ways that uphold our values.

IN CLOSING

Intuition and reflection are critical boundary-setting skills. They are tools that many people have been taught to doubt, minimize, or ignore. Part of developing vibrant, creative, and flexible boundaries that reflect who and how we are in the world is having a support system that grows with us, challenges us, nurtures us, and offers constructive reality checks. Having these kinds of support systems helps people learn to identify and listen to intuition in complex and grounded ways. The REFLECTIVE LOOP is a dynamic, holonic life resource. The more we integrate some kind of reflective loop into our lives and relationships, the more expansive and resilient our boundaries can be. Critical intuition and a reflective loop help people navigate obstacles and barriers to boundary setting. The next chapter considers goals, objectives, and some challenges in boundary setting.

FIVE

GOALS AND CHALLENGES IN SETTING, DEFENDING, OR NEGOTIATING BOUNDARIES

CLARIFYING GOALS

THERE ARE MANY REASONS TO SET BOUNDARIES. SOMETIMES OUR GOAL in setting a boundary is obvious. Other times we may have competing or conflicting goals and there may even be situations where we are not sure what our goal is. It can be helpful, when possible, to be clear about your goal(s) for setting a boundary. Being aware of your goals for a boundary will inform how and when you may choose to use different skills. For the purposes of this book, we will explore three goals or objectives for a boundary. The first goal is to have the boundary adhered to no matter what. Whether or not someone agrees with, understands, likes, or respects the boundary, putting it out there and having it followed is the primary goal. The second goal is having your boundary consented to because it is agreed upon and understood. The third goal is sticking to your values or belief system, or maintaining a sense of self-respect. There will be times when we will want to meet all three goals and are able to. There will be other times when we may need to prioritize one over the other. Knowing your primary objectives beforehand helps to prioritize and guide boundary work when necessary. While the objectives are not always mutually exclusive, there are times when being effective means choosing one.

A class participant struggling to navigate and set boundaries in a shared living situation offers an example of the first goal, having your boundary respected regardless of if the person likes or agrees with it:

There are six of us living together and we share a lot of things—food, clothes, tools. We borrow one another's things all the time. Mostly I was fine with this and we all worked on negotiating how to share amongst us. But I didn't want people coming in my room when I wasn't at home. When I told my roommates that they were not allowed in my room when I was not there, it was not up for negotiation. I didn't want them to be upset or hurt, but some of them were. I had to deal with a few of them being confused and hurt. They really didn't understand my boundary and took it personally, but like I said, it wasn't up for a discussion. This was my boundary and it needed to be accepted, even if they didn't understand or agree with it.

The second goal, having the boundary agreed upon, is, to a great degree, about maintaining or tending to relationships. The goal in this case involves both the boundary itself and the relationship, and prioritizes having mutual understanding of, and consent to, the boundary. Another client shares how he and his girlfriend navigated such a situation. His goal was to have an agreement about communication while he was gone on tour to talk once a day. His girlfriend felt like that was not enough contact and wanted to be able to call him whenever she felt like it. It was important for her that she felt good about any agreement they made and he also felt strongly about his boundary (to talk once a day unless it was an emergency):

My band is on tour a few times a year. It's hard to be on the road, playing a show almost every night and keep your focus. There is always drama and the way I deal is to shut everything that isn't necessary out. I love my girlfriend and talking to her when I get up sets me in a good space for the rest of the day. But when I talk to her multiple times a day it makes it harder for me to be in the mental space I need to be in to get through the tour. I know it's hard for her to understand this and not feel like I am shutting her out. We talked a lot about it and I tried to get her to understand that it was actually about me wanting to be fully present when we talk. I can do that once a day but more than that and I am not really there, I am in my head and scattered. After talking about it, she got it. I am not sure she totally understands, but gets it enough to feel okay about it. That was huge for me. I wanted her to be on board, to feel good [and] not like I was doing something that hurt her.

In this example, the goal was agreeing to a boundary, not just having the boundary itself respected. My client may have handled the situation differently if his goal was to have his boundary set and respected, whether or not his girlfriend liked or understood it. Knowing your goal can be helpful. If someone disagrees with your boundary and the goal is to have it respected no matter what, the approach and what gets focused on may be very different than if someone disagrees with your boundary and the goal is to have them feel good about it. In some situations, there will be room for negotiation and collaboration, in others there will not be. It is important to be aware that one can be compassionate and empathic while refusing to negotiate a boundary. In the previous example of setting a boundary with roommates, the class participant can offer sympathy to her roommates' struggle to understand her boundary without changing it. She can be compassionate about any hurt feelings, acknowledge and validate them, again without changing her boundary. There may be situations in which you will want to change or renegotiate your boundary based on people's reaction to it. There will also be times when you will not want to alter your boundary. There will be many times when we want both of these things (have our boundary agreed upon and respected) and yet they are not possible for a variety of reasons. In these situations, it can be helpful to be aware of your primary objective. What is more important, having the boundary set and adhered to or maintaining the relationship? Is there room for negotiating and collaboration around the boundary? Is the boundary flexible? Is the relationship more important than the boundary?

In other situations, your goal may be to stick to your values and belief system. You may value loyalty, for example, and believe it is important to have a friend's back even if they are doing something you don't agree with. Another client discusses his decision to support a friend of his who was lying to his boyfriend, even though he himself values honesty:

> My friend told me he had been lying to his partner, not telling him that he was still using pills. I told him he needed to come clean about it and he said, "Not yet." He was working on it, but not ready. It was a tough situation for me. I am not super close with his boyfriend but I also have a strict policy of not lying to friends and he put me in a position where I might have to choose between my values and backing him up. Thankfully it never came to that. I would have backed my friend up, but it would have been rough. I don't like lying and being in that position felt like it was a compromise of my values.

There are plenty of times where your goal will be to set boundaries and keep a relationship while staying rooted in personal values. However, given the complexities of life and interpersonal situations, this may not always be possible. Knowing what is more (and sometimes most) important, even if it's only a little more and only for that particular moment, helps ground and guide boundary work. Another client shares an example of having to be clear on their goals and making an informed decision on how to prioritize them;

> I let my family know that they needed to use my correct pronoun. Of course I cared if they were upset and wanted them to not only support me and use the right pronoun, but [to also] do it with love and be happy for me. But thinking about my priorities, I made it clear that if they were struggling or having a hard time, it wasn't my job to make it okay or let them off the hook. This was not easy for me. But being able to recognize for myself how important it was to hold that boundary and not change it because they felt uncomfortable was good.

ASPECTS TO CONSIDER

Below are some things to consider when deciding if you need to prioritize your goals. Some of the goals and aspects to consider when setting boundaries are in part informed by Marsha Linehan's interpersonal effectiveness skills from her Dialectical Behavioral Therapy work. Reflecting on these factors can help tease out context and may be useful in assessing whether to set a boundary and if so, how it might be set. This is most certainly not an exhaustive list, but a place to start. It is not necessary to reflect on each aspect every time a boundary is being set; different ones will be helpful in different contexts.

SAFETY: Are you emotionally, physically, mentally safe? Will your or someone else's safety be affected if you use a boundary-setting skill?

IMPORTANCE: How important is the boundary to you?

RESOURCES/ACCESS/CAPACITY: Do I have the emotional, mental, physical, spiritual, means or resources to set the boundary? Do the people involved have the means/resources to address my boundary/needs?

AUTHORITY: Do I have authority over the person? Do they have authority over me? How does authority inform or impact my boundary work in this situation?

POWER: Do I have social, personal, emotional, economic, or political power over the person? Do they have power over me? How does power inform or impact my boundary work in this situation?

EVIDENCE AND FACTS: Do I know everything I need to know to decide whether to set a boundary and if so, how to set it?

IMMEDIATE, SHORT- AND LONG-TERM GOALS: What are they? How do they connect to each other? Is one more important? If so, is it important to consider why?

CONTEXT: Is this a good time to set a boundary? Is this boundary appropriate to the relationship and context? Is it what I really want for the relationship? Do I have a right to set the boundary?

VALUES: Does the boundary work within my values system? If not, how do I feel about that?

INTENTION: What is the intention of setting this boundary?

RECIPROCITY: Am I giving as well as taking, listening as well as talking, protecting myself as well as thinking of the well-being of others?

CHALLENGES: BOUNDARIES, REACTIONS, AND FEELINGS

Things often do not occur as one would have hoped, and life (with its associated boundaries) does not always go as planned. Sometimes people's reactions to boundaries prompt intense feelings of guilt (*I should not have set the boundary*), shame (*I am a bad/selfish person for setting the boundary*), anxiety (*something bad is going to happen as a result of setting the boundary*), or resentment (*they should just be able to respect my boundary*). These feelings can impact the boundary and often get conflated with the boundary itself. If someone feels remorse about setting a boundary, this may lead them to believe the boundary is bad or wrong. Or they may interpret a person's reaction of disappointment as evidence that their boundary is unacceptable. For example, if someone feels guilty about saying no to a friend, when they do set the boundary (No) and their friend becomes upset, they may see this as evidence that their boundary is bad, rather than understanding their boundary is still acceptable (but in this case, also hurtful for someone they care about).

It is helpful to learn to separate the boundary itself from the feelings one has about setting it and also from the feelings and thoughts about people's responses to it. The more skilled one becomes at recognizing these different elements in boundary setting, the more options there are in navigating them. One can tend to the other person's feelings about a boundary while still upholding it. Continuing with the above example, if someone says no and hurts a friend's feelings, the boundary setter can still be compassionate with themselves for feeling guilty and empathetic toward their friend without changing their boundary. They may even want to invite their friend to discuss his or her feelings, independent from the boundary itself: "I know you are upset. Is there anything that I or we can do to make you feel better without changing my boundary?"

People sometimes believe that if a boundary hurts or makes them or the other person feel bad in any manner, the boundary itself is not acceptable. For example, take a couple that lives together. One partner hates having people stop by unannounced and wants to set a boundary that people call first to arrange a time. And the other partner loves having a home where friends can drop by without calling, and feels sad and even depressed about the boundary their partner wants to set, potentially causing them to push back against the boundary. A lot of different feelings can be triggered when a boundary hurts or distresses someone you care about. Having the capacity to separate the boundary from the associated reactions and feelings to it, as well as reactions and feelings to the reactions and feelings (yours and other people's), can help people make more grounded choices about how they want to navigate the situation. There are many possibilities. One approach is to collaborate about how to address the issue while maintaining the boundary. Another is to renegotiate the boundary itself. The reality is that our boundaries will make us and other people feel all sorts of emotions. This is part of boundary work and not to be avoided. Rather, learning how to set boundaries and grapple with the accompanying emotions is what deepens and expands boundary work to include all kinds of boundaries adaptive to different contexts and needs.

CHALLENGES: THE MYTH OF "GOOD" BOUNDARY SETTING

It is not unusual to mistake people's resistance to a boundary as a lack of clear communication. This tends to occur because people often believe that a "good" boundary is a clear boundary and a clear boundary is one that people will respect or respond to. The reality is, we have no control over how people respond to our boundaries. While we can, and most certainly do, use information and knowledge about someone to inform how we communicate a boundary, this does not translate into controlling how the person will respond. When people do not respond in the manner we expected or hoped, reflecting on what contributed to creating conditions where such responses occurred can be helpful. This reflection is done in the spirit of compassionate curiosity, not as a way to shame or judge others or ourselves. Reflecting offers us a way to explore and develop an understanding of the varying complex contexts in which boundaries are set rather than seek a formulaic approach or reductive answer. Consider the example from a class participant:

I never realized that when I asked for something, I approached it as if the person was already going to disagree. So I would preemptively argue my point. Instead of asking my girlfriend to pick up after herself because I hate coming home and having stuff dropped everywhere, I would talk about how being messy is not okay or how having a house that is clean is important to a relationship. I realized I was trying to frontload any discussion with reasons why I was right. She, of course, would disagree because she doesn't care about having things picked up all the time. It could get kind of mean at times. I'd call her messy and she'd call me uptight. This didn't help. When I stopped trying to convince her I was right and asked for what I needed by sharing how I felt, it worked out better. She was able to see how having things picked up made me feel less stressed at the end of the day, which benefited her because I was more relaxed. This actually motivated her to try to pick up more, which I love, and it made me more able to let a few things go because I saw how much she was trying.

In the following example, a woman in a self-defense class explores her experience in a challenging situation:

I was walking home from work. It was late at night and this guy approached me asking what time it was. I had this funny feeling, but ignored it because he was young and didn't look very scary. I told him the time and when he didn't walk away, I got a little scared. I wasn't sure what to do so I said good night, sort of dismissing him. I didn't want to walk away and turn my back to him. He stood there and I realized he was assessing me and the situation. I also realized I needed to set a bigger boundary, really let him know he didn't want to mess with me. I put up my hands and said good night again, only more firm and louder. He nodded and started backing up, saying something like, "Okay, cool," or something like that. I stayed where I was until he was down the block and turned the corner.

In both of these situations people changed how they were setting boundaries in reaction to how people responded to them. They both paid attention to their internal experience, what the other person was doing, and were mindful of the context. Being aware of how we communicate boundaries and the impact we have on others is important, but it does not translate into the ability to control how people will respond. The idea that if we set good and clear boundaries, people will respond the way we want is a myth based in fear and victim blaming. In the above example, it can be easy to assume the man walked away because she set a good, clear boundary. However, the reality is that we have no idea why the man walked away. Assuming he walked away because she set a clear boundary implies that if he had instead chosen to try to mug or assault her, it would have been because she didn't set a clear boundary. This puts blame and responsibility for what happens on her rather than on the man who is making decisions about whether or not to walk away, and makes the conditions in which this is happening invisible.

People's responses to a boundary are not necessarily a good gauge as to how well or how clearly a boundary was communicated. Sometimes a boundary is communicated beautifully, but the person does not want or like the boundary and so resists it. They may get mad, or express hurt, and want the boundary to change. Sometimes it feels okay to change a boundary. Other times, it does not. Sometimes resistance to a boundary feels really bad; in other situations, pushback may not affect us much, if at all. If your supervisor becomes angry when you try to set a boundary about how much work you can take on, it may have more of an emotional impact than if your three-year-old gets upset because it's bedtime. If our partner resists our boundary around having people call before they stop by, it may open up larger discussions about what "home" means to both people and how to navigate differences.

A person's reaction to a boundary offers information to be considered. Whether or not a boundary is renegotiated depends on a variety of elements and the context in which the boundary is being set. The more we move away from the myth that a good boundary is one that is clear and therefore respected, the more we can be mindful of all the various aspects and conditions that make up a boundary-setting scenario.

POWER AND INTENTION

Two important factors in setting, defending, and negotiating boundaries are power and intention. If you have the power and the ability to renegotiate your boundary, then renegotiation can be a wonderful part of personal and relational growth. If you don't have, or don't believe you have, the power or ability to renegotiate, then it's not necessarily a negotiation. This does not mean that boundaries are not being set. Power informs how people will identify, communicate, and defend boundaries. There are a myriad of ways that people set limits in very challenging situations. An important part of boundary work is identifying the ways we set limits in various contexts and how power informs our decisions. Boundaries are very personal and adaptable. A friend shares an example from his childhood, growing up as a survivor of abuse:

When I was a kid my life was pretty chaotic. There were a lot of different people going in and out of the house I lived in. There was a lot of partying and people crashing at the house. Some of them did things to me that I didn't like. They would hit me or kiss me or make me sit on their lap and touch me, but when I said something or tried to walk away they would joke about how I needed to toughen up and laugh at me when I cried. At some point, I learned that it wasn't going to help me to say anything to them, or to my dad who told me the same thing: toughen up and shut up. So I fought back the only way I could—I would pretend I didn't hear them when they called me, I would freeze like a zombie when they touched me, I peed in their gas tanks, stole money out of their wallets when they were sleeping, that sort of thing.

People set boundaries and defend themselves in extraordinary ways that can be minimized or not even noticed if the context is not considered. Boundaries that are set in one context will be very different in another. In thinking about the ways that power and intention inform boundary work, it can be helpful to reflect on different times in your life and note the various boundary-setting, self-care, and coping strategies you used, and consider how or if these may be informing how you set and communicate boundaries presently.

CHANGING THE LENS

Being in a situation where someone can and does cross boundaries does not mean that people give up having the boundaries or using self-defense skills. Sometimes, as in the example above, people set really badass boundaries that are crossed simply because other people have the power and ability to do so. It can be helpful and empowering to recognize the boundary setting, self-care, and self-defense that people use even in situations where boundary crossing and harm happen. Doing this can help mitigate victim blaming and the stigma of guilt, blame, and shame. A class participant shares her experience with domestic violence:

I used to be really embarrassed that I had been in an abusive relationship. After talking in class about all the things I did to survive and finally leave, I feel proud of myself. I never thought about what I did, all the ways I fought back, resisted what was happening, and how much I tried to keep my head together. I blamed myself for not seeing the warning signs and not leaving earlier. It made me feel a lot less ashamed when I was able to see the things I did [do], like lying, hiding things, pretending I liked something, or even provoking her at times just to get it over with, as survival strategies and even as me setting boundaries in a messed up situation.

For survivors of interpersonal violence, sexual abuse, domestic violence, date rape, sexual harassment and bullying, identifying which self-defense, self-care, and boundary-setting skills were used to survive the incident(s) can be helpful. The myth that setting a clear boundary means it will also be respected can lead survivors of violence to blame themselves. It can require a lot of support to let go of the myth that you can change power dynamics and cultural norms (which support and create conditions in which many forms of violence are tolerated, ignored, or even encouraged) with good boundary setting or a badass self-defense strategy. Stop asking yourself, *why didn't I do this or that?* and instead replace it with, *what did I do to survive?*

Sometimes bad things happen despite our best efforts. How we think about these events shapes how we remember them and how we feel about ourselves. Changing the framework or lens through which events are viewed changes self-talk and the emotional responses to the events. Letting go of asking yourself, *what should I have done to prevent X, Y, or Z from happening?* and instead asking, *what did I do to get through X, Y, or Z?* changes the lens. It is also possible to explore why we responded the way we did without blame or shame by using compassionate curiosity. The *Why* then, is no longer connected to a sense of responsibility, but rather becomes a way to consider what factors or conditions contributed to the decisions that were made. A class participant shares:

I was date raped when I was in my early twenties. Whenever I remembered that night, I always had this mental list of things I should have done. I really beat myself up with that list. In class, when we talked about looking at things you did do rather than what you should have done, I saw all these things that I ignored or told myself were not import-ant because they didn't prevent the assault. Now when I think about it, I still wish it didn't happen, but I don't blame myself. I can see all the things I did to try to prevent it, get through it, and deal with it after-ward—those are all boundary-setting and self-defense skills. I am more understanding with myself about why I made the decisions I did.

Boundary work can involve renegotiating how we recall, remember, and tell stories about events, which impacts how we feel about them. Changing how we feel about an event informs how we remember it, which transforms our relationship to it. This process can change shame-ful and triggering memories into painful but also empowering ones, or even simply transform the negative memories that no longer have the power to induce distressing and overwhelming emotions. In self-defense and boundary-setting classes I saw this happen time after time as people recalled traumatic events while staying present enough to be able to identify boundary-setting and self-defense skills they may not have rec-ognized before. A class participant shares a powerful example of moving from shame to feeling empowered by her decisions in a horrific situation:

When I was in high school I was abducted and raped. For years, I blamed myself. I didn't scream or fight back. I agreed to everything he said and did. When we did the exercise in class, it was a struggle for me to see what I did as active boundary setting or self-defense. How was not fighting back self-defense? But over time I realized that what I was doing was making the best decision for how I thought I could survive. These were active decisions that I was making based on my situation and my best understanding of what would keep me alive. It wasn't easy but over time I stopped blaming myself and worked on seeing my actions as choices and that my choices kept me alive.

There are a number of factors that inform how people will set boundaries across a range of situations: skill, capacity, resources, past experiences, cultural norms, personality, circumstances, and information, just to name a few. All of these influence decisions about boundaries. Rather than blame ourselves for what we did or did not do in a particular instance, it can be more useful to explore all the various dynamics that informed how we decided to navigate our situation. This can be done while still holding others and ourselves accountable, and while exploring alternative options. For example, if I set a boundary in a situation by lying even though I value honesty, I can explore which factors influenced my decision (with compassion), and hold myself accountable for lying while seeing if there are alternative options available for similar situations in the future.

The Role of Thoughts, Emotions, and Interpretations in Boundary Setting

Sometimes the emotions that arise in anticipation of a particular reaction to a boundary can trigger preemptive feelings and reactions. For example, if someone is anxious about receiving an angry response to their boundary, they may feel defensive even before engaging in any boundary setting. A client shares an example about realizing he was anticipating a response from his girlfriend without realizing it:

> *I figured she would be really angry that I wanted to take separate vacations this year. That [thought] freaked me out. I got totally prepared for an angry response. I was defensive and had all kinds of justifications about why she shouldn't be angry and why it wasn't that bad that I wanted time alone, why it was healthily, normal, etc. I was so focused on my "defense," that it took me a while to realize she wasn't angry. She was hurt and me telling her why she shouldn't be upset was hurting her more. I wasn't able to really listen to her at first. If I had come to the conversation more open about finding out how she felt rather than assuming she would be angry and responding to her as if she was angry, it probably would have gone much better.*

Being intentional with boundaries requires listening to ourselves and to others. The emotional response to an anticipated reaction of a boundary can cloud our approach. It can make it difficult to be fully present and to really discover how the other person is feeling and reacting. If someone is ready for a certain response, they look for it, which means focus and attention are directed toward a specific reaction and more often than not, people find it even if it is not there. People interpret events through the lens of thoughts and emotions. Thoughts and emotions (specifically anxiety and worry, in the above example about an angry reaction) frame how events are seen and interpreted. In the previous example, the client's defensiveness made it difficult to recognize that his partner's reactions were not expressions of anger, but of disappointment.

Taking the time to cultivate an internal awareness of how thoughts and emotions frame events, and how events are seen and interpreted, helps people to be more present in the moment. Being more present means being able to respond to what is actually happening, rather than to an interpretation based on certain thoughts and emotions. Approaching situations in this way also increases capacity and skill around clarification. Being aware that you are fearful of an angry response to your boundary while being mindful that your fear informs how reactions are interpreted offers you the room needed to tend to the feelings, to check in and clarify. Using the above example again, if my client had been aware of his anxiety before entering into the conversation about his desire to have separate vacations, he could have used self-soothing skills, asked his partner for reassurance, or chosen to clarify by asking her if she was angry. If he was aware that his fear of an angry response was fueling his anxiety, he could tend to his fear directly rather than trying to eliminate it by getting his partner to agree with him. Doing this separates the feeling (fear) from the boundary (taking a separate vacation). He was anxious about the response to his boundary, not the boundary itself. When we are able to tease out the different elements (feelings, thoughts, reactions to boundaries, and the feelings and thoughts they elicit), there is more room to tend to them. This allows us to be more responsive and less reactive. It also creates space to be able to maintain the boundary while tending to the impact that setting the boundary has. A client talks about her experience with this in her relationship when she made a decision to take a job in another city:

> *When I stopped focusing so much on trying to make sure she didn't get sad about my decision to take a new job in a different city, I was able to really listen to her and make space for her sadness. Before, I felt so guilty about making the decision to move that I kept trying to make her feel better so I wouldn't feel guilty. But all this did was make her feel like I didn't care. I got hurt and defensive because I do care and turned it on her—that if she cared, she would be happy for me. We kept going in circles. Then it hit me, I could be compassionate about her sadness without feeling like that means I should change my decision.*

People can be compassionate and loving while setting boundaries that are unpopular or hurtful, even if holding onto a boundary is interpreted as not being compassionate. Sometimes people don't like the boundaries that are being set. That's okay. Sometimes boundaries are renegotiated, other times they are not. Sometimes it is important to really take the time to understand and validate the person's feelings about a boundary (which doesn't mean the boundary needs to be changed). Other times it is not as important to do this. The conditions under which boundaries are being set shape and inform how people will choose to act and respond.

NAVIGATING NEGATIVE RESPONSES

When people don't like a boundary, they sometimes try to change it by demonstrating the potentially negative impact it may have. "If you don't let me borrow your bike, I won't have any way to get home." "There is no one else who can do this project, you can't quit now."

"I don't want you to take that job. It will put more stress on both of us." "My sister will kill me if we don't go see her when we are in town." "I'm scared to go to the doctor alone, I want you to go with me to my appointment." "When you tell me you can't talk right now, I feel abandoned." "When you refuse to change how you talk to me, it makes it really hard to listen to you." Explaining the impact of a boundary is neither good nor bad. Sometimes discovering the impact of a boundary leads to a renegotiation or change in the boundary. Other times it does not. Sometimes it is important or can be helpful to understand the impact of a boundary. Context is important. A class participant shares an example of when she and her partner got caught up in trying to explain the impact of a behavior as a way to set or change a boundary:

My partner and I are different. Really different. I come from a loud family that talks a lot, talks over one another, and we are always doing other things when we have conversations. She comes from what I'll call a more reserved family. Just her mom and her, and they both are quiet. When we have discussions or arguments, she can't stand it when I get distracted or say something that doesn't seem directly related. Then we get into a fight about that, about her thinking I am not listening because I start fidgeting with something or get up.

For a long time she told me how this made her feel unimportant, which would make me upset but also defensive. I didn't mean to shut her down and don't think the way I listen is bad. It's like we talked about in class— she kept trying to show me the negative impact of the way I listen, hoping that I would change my boundary (which I guess was me saying I listen better when I am doing something with my hands and I didn't want to change that even if I could). We ended up trying to see if there was any way she could believe she was important to me and that I was listening, even if I was doing something with my hands or moving around. It was not easy and we are still struggling with this, but we are working on it.

Sometimes boundaries are renegotiated in response to the impact they have on people. A friend discusses a situation where she changed her boundary:

My boyfriend and I had been working to pay off a lot of debt, and at the time, we were both working two jobs. He really wanted to quit one, but we both were scared we would never get the debt paid off if we didn't keep on track. I also felt like if he quit one, I shouldn't have to keep working two jobs, but we couldn't afford that. After a lot of talks where he was able to get me to see how much his second job was really messing him up, how we could make a plan for me to quit one of my jobs in the not-too-distant future and how our relationship was suffering, I was able to see his side.

Context is important. There are a multitude of elements that go into boundary setting and boundary negotiation. In addition to the list of "Aspects to Consider," there are our thoughts and feelings about the boundary, thoughts and feelings about other people's (real or perceived) responses to the boundary, and thoughts and feelings about our response to their response. There is much to navigate when setting boundaries. Again, using supports systems, check-ins, self-reflection, and compassionate curiosity can enhance this work.

SIX

COMPASSION AND BOUNDARIES

To Suffer With

How do we deal with people's reactions to our boundaries? How do we not give in when they hook, manipulate, push, or prod us into giving up our boundaries? How do we not connect their reaction with our right to set a boundary? How do we do this with grace and groundedness? There isn't one right way, but examining the powerful skill of compassion can help us answer these questions. Cultivating compassion, empathy, and understanding for people's reactions (and our reactions to their reactions) to boundaries can be immensely helpful. Compassion and self-directed compassion help people be less reactive and more responsive to events (boundaries, thoughts, feelings, other people's behaviors and actions, etc.).

Reacting is immediate; there is no pause or reflection, and it tends to be emotionally driven and often defensive. Reacting is important. There are times when we need to act decisively, quickly, and without reflection. Responding involves taking the time (pause) to look at the situation at hand, consider the circumstances and context, and reflect on what is happening before deciding on any action. The pause could be for any length of time, a couple of seconds, a few hours, days—the amount of time will vary; what is important is the pause itself. The pause signals to the body that one is not in immediate and impending danger (even if in an emotionally distressing situation) and places one in a more mindful space. Having the ability to choose to respond rather than react is an important skill and one that people can develop over time. The pause can start with a single breath; taking a walk; counting to ten; letting yourself emote before responding; taking time to write, draw, or dance; or reflecting on the situation in some way by playing loud music, praying, or singing; or talking with a mentor—the possibilities are endless and as unique as each of us. Responding allows one to consider and be empathetic to themselves as well as other people's perspectives and feelings. It is important to not mistake compassion for needing to change a boundary. People can be compassionate and demonstrate empathy without changing their boundaries. Sometimes this *is* the most compassionate thing. What is compassion? According to the Vietnamese Buddhist monk Thich Nhat Hanh:

> *The essence of love and compassion is understanding, the ability to recognize the physical, material, and psychological suffering of others, to put ourselves "inside the skin" of the other. We "go inside" their body, feelings, and mental formations, and witness for ourselves their suffering. Shallow observation as an outsider is not enough to see their suffering. We must become one with the subject of our observation. When we are in contact with another's suffering, or our own suffering, a feeling of compassion is born in us. Compassion means, literally, "to suffer with."* [8]

Recognizing, acknowledging, and validating another person's pain and suffering (or our own) is powerful, and yet most of us struggle to do this well, especially when we are the ones who have caused the pain. It

---

[8]   Hesselink, Katinka. "Thich Nhat Hanh: Short Quotes on Love and Compassion." http://www.katinkahesselink.net/tibet/Thich-Nhat-Hanh-love-q.html.

is easy to react in situations where we are (or think we are) responsible for someone else's pain by trying to make them feel better rather than responding by simply witnessing their suffering. Self-directed compassion simply means directing compassion toward ourselves. While the concept of self-directed compassion is fairly straightforward, the process and skill of turning toward ourselves with compassion can be challenging. We are often harder on ourselves than we are on anyone else.

There is a German phrase that a mentor of mine shared with me years ago that translates roughly as, "That causes me pain." The phrase *Es tut mir Leid* is often used in situations where American English speakers might say, "I am sorry." The German expression prompts you to recognize the suffering of the other person as well as the pain their suffering causes you. It keeps the focus on the person who has been hurt while recognizing the ripple effect of their pain. All too often, the focus is on how to make the person (or us) feel better without any real recognition of their suffering. The idea of *Es tut mir Leid* in this context is to hold more compassionate space for suffering (our own as well as other people's) without jumping in and trying to fix, soothe, or alleviate it.

How could the concept of "suffering with" help boundary work? Having compassion for the impact a boundary may have without necessarily needing to change the boundary makes our boundary stronger. Having compassion for ourselves as we set, maintain, negotiate, explain, and sometimes defend boundaries makes boundary work a richer experience. Without compassion and self-directed compassion, it is easy to victim blame, shame, and judge ourselves or others for responses to boundaries, and even the boundaries themselves. Judgment, blame, and shame make boundary work harder. Accountability, compassionate curiosity, and reflection strengthen boundary work, even as they allow boundaries to be more flexible and adaptive to changing contexts. A class participant shares:

I used to beat myself up pretty bad. I had a hard time saying no to people. I would say yes to the point where I felt used, then I would get mad and resentful with the other person for taking advantage of me, even though

I was the one saying yes to everything. It was hard to sort out my feelings and other people's feelings. If I said no and they were disappointed, I felt like a horrible person. Rather than say no, I would spend time and energy trying to get them to change their mind about something I didn't want to do. Then when they didn't, I would think they were being stubborn or arrogant or inflexible. The better I got at saying no and being okay with people's reactions, even when they were disappointed (which was hard), the less I judged them for their feelings and the less I judged myself when it was hard to set boundaries.

We can be accountable for the impact our boundary has without changing it. We can be compassionate with ourselves for our feelings about people's responses to our boundary, which in turn makes it easier to tend to those feelings rather than trying to not feel them at all. Compassion and self-directed compassion increase our capacity and skill with boundaries. This does not mean we always have to feel compassionate toward someone or act in a compassionate way in every situation. There may be times when we do not. That is fine. A class participant shares an important moment of non-compassionate reaction in a very horrible situation. She had been attacked while walking home and her attacker was trying to drag her off the street she was on:

When I kicked my attacker, punched him in the face and throat, I didn't see him as a person. I didn't think about that at all. I couldn't. When I realized it was either him or me, something in me flipped a switch and in that moment, I chose me. I didn't care about him at all.

A client shares another example of needing to renegotiate their relationship with compassion in order to take care of themselves:

A few months after extricating myself from a super codependent relationship, I realized that it was my compassion and empathy and guilt that had made me feel stuck. If I hurt my partner or caused him pain in any way, I felt awful and tried to figure out a way to not do whatever it was. I stopped going to school, stopped talking to my friends, stopped dressing the way I used to. A lot of people wanted me to feel mad at him. I did for a while but that felt bad, too. It took a long time to really come to terms with the reality that I can feel compassion and still do something that hurts someone else. I needed to be angry at him for a while in order to get the hell out of there. But then, it felt important for me to not keep hating him. I wanted to feel compassion, but not let that pull me into changing how I want to be in the world.

It is important to separate feeling compassion and empathy from the boundaries we need to set, the actions we need to take, and the decisions necessary in life. We can be compassionate to the pain our actions cause while remaining grounded in the reality that we still need to take that action. There will be times when we cause suffering and we will choose to change our behavior, and there will be times when we will not want to change our actions despite the pain they cause. Compassion allows us to make more informed, more intentional choices about our boundaries.

WHEN WE CAUSE SUFFERING

In our lives we will get hurt and we will inevitably hurt other people. Hurting and being hurt is unavoidable; how we do it is not. If I say no to someone and they take it personally and get hurt, I can be compassionate to their suffering without changing my boundary. I can hold onto my no with an open heart and mind. I can do this even when their hurt is huge because my boundary is necessary. In fact, having compassion without getting hooked is what allows us to not get distracted from our boundary by the need to justify, explain, or defend it. A workshop participant shares:

As a mom, this really began to resonate with me. I saw how I would be impatient with other adults but not as much with my daughter. When I said no to her and she didn't like it or agree, I was fine explaining and also fine if she didn't like it and got upset. But I realized I wasn't fine if my partner was disappointed or upset when I said no about something. I got frustrated, even angry, because I wanted him to feel differently about my boundary. Not only did I want him to respect my boundary, I wanted him to understand, agree, and not have any negative feelings about it.

The capacity to have compassion while holding clear boundaries is an important interpersonal skill. When there is disagreement or misunderstanding about a boundary, it can be challenging to approach the interaction with compassion. But having compassion creates more spaciousness and offers more opportunities for creative problem-solving because things are less likely to become polarized. Compassion interrupts the polarization process. Some of the elements about the polarization process are pulled from John Gottman's work on couples and relationships (www.gottman.com). In this context, polarization is about conflicts over boundaries (i.e., different boundaries or different desires for boundaries). The conflict over a boundary (one person wants the boundary and the other person does not) sparks an effort for change simultaneously alongside an effort for maintenance. In other words, one person defends the boundary and the other person attempts to change it. The attempt to change produces a counteraction (defense of the boundary). The resulting polarization occurs because each person's defense of his or her position escalates the other person's need to defend his or her counter position. The way out of polarization is compassion for the other person's experience. Compassion may or may not result in any change in the boundary itself, but takes people out of the escalating polarization cycle. A client shares an example:

My husband and I just couldn't get out of this cycle. I wanted him to understand why I didn't want to give up going to the gym before work and why it was important to be able to hang out with coworkers after work sometimes. I work a lot and both of those things help me stay focused and not burn out. He wanted me to be at home more with him and our daughter. From his perspective, I was being selfish. I thought he was being stubborn and not supportive of me doing the things that help me be a better partner. We were at an impasse, with neither of us giving an inch. When I started trying to be compassionate to his position, things started to change. I was able to see where he was coming from, [acknowledge] his feelings and concerns. He wanted to spend time together as a family, which was actually something I wanted as well. Once I realized that we wanted the same thing but had different means of getting there, it was easier for me to not polarize things. I was able to say we both want to spend time as a family, and I need to have time with friends and at the gym. From that place, we were able to see both of our needs as important and figure out a compromise.

It's easier to listen, understand, and learn when one is not guarded or defended. It is challenging to not be defensive when someone points out how a behavior is causing them harm or explaining why they dislike it. And, it can be challenging to let someone know in a compassionate way that they are doing something you dislike or that is causing discomfort or harm. Sometimes people confuse compassion with being soft with boundaries. This is another myth about boundaries. It is possible to let someone know with absolute loving kindness that what is being said or done is hurtful, distressing, or unacceptable. Without compassion, it can be easy to fall into a justification trap where someone believes they have to defend their boundary because if they demonstrate compassion they will be forced to give it up. When a boundary is armed with justifications and explanations, it can spark and perpetuate defensiveness and counter-defensiveness on all sides, leading to escalation and polarization. A client shares an example:

My partner is a processer. She likes to talk everything out. Me, I think you can just say what you need to say and then move on. We used to do the polarization a lot. She would tell me why I needed to talk about my feelings more. I'd get defensive or shut down because it seemed like no matter what I did, it was never enough. The more she pushed to talk, the more I shut down. It was a bad cycle. I'd try to point out why she should leave things alone or let them go, and she'd get defensive and want to talk about that. We dug ourselves into a big hole with both of us feeling attacked, hurt, not listened to, and really alone and far away from each other.

Compassion and self-directed compassion increase the capacity to listen, which increases the opportunities to be heard. This, in turn, increases the capacity to accept other people's experiences even when they diverge or are in conflict from our own. The capacity to listen and accept even when disagreeing is a powerful way to interrupt the polarization process. It creates room for a boundary to be set and maintained, disagreed with, and problem solved around—all important boundary-negotiation skills. Continuing with the above example:

… Once we both learned how to be compassionate to one another and toward ourselves, things changed. I tried to understand how hard it was for her to not process, that her desire to talk things out was something I respected about her and even though it was hard for me, it was something to respect and value about her. I also felt like she tried to understand my need to not talk about things. I could see this was hard for her and the more compassionate I was about this, the easier it was for me to be nice and loving toward her struggle with my need to end the conversation while also keeping my boundary.

This couple learned how to navigate and negotiate differences in their boundaries, in this case about wants and needs in regard to processing events in their relationship.

THE ART OF NEGOTIATION

Negotiation is an art and a skill that we hone over time, with practice. It's not a simple or easy thing. Negotiation is often viewed as a compromise between two parties with both people focused on getting as much of what they want as possible. This is one definition of negotiation that comes primarily from capitalism and market ideology. The principles of negotiation for our purposes are: negotiation as a dialogue between parties intended to reach an understanding; resolving points of difference; or, producing an agreement upon courses of action. From this framework, one can set a boundary and negotiate with someone about how to handle the impact of it, or work to resolve how to manage the boundary within the relationship without changing the boundary itself. Of course, negotiation of a boundary may also mean changing the boundary itself—but the process of negotiation is about communication and understanding, not necessarily about changing the boundary so that everyone agrees to it.

Our boundaries, like ourselves, change and grow constantly. Things we once needed to have firmly in place in order to feel safe, we may let go of. Lines we once drew to clearly designate where not to cross may change and be redrawn as we understand more about the world we live in and our place in it. Our boundaries will change as we develop a more complex view of our world, our relationships, and our wants and needs. This is healthy and normal. People will be upset with us when we set limits, and feelings will get hurt when we say something someone does not want to hear. This is inevitable. We can let this hinder our ability to set boundaries, or we can let this knowledge inform how we interact with the effects of our boundaries. It's a choice. People's responses to our boundaries give us information. Our reaction to their responses gives us even more information. The more informed we are, the better choices we can make. The more complex our understanding becomes, the harder it is to rely on polarized victim blaming and reactive rationales. This means we have to assume more personal responsibility for the needs and desires that inform our boundaries. Being accountable is fabulous, scary, exciting, daunting, and tremendously important. We are the experts in what we want and need, and we are the only ones who can set boundaries around it. No one can do this work for us.

In the next section, we will explore social contexts that inform boundaries and self-care. Being our own expert in what we want and need and being accountable for this is an ongoing process and evolution that involves learning, listening, communicating, and a deep understanding of the myriad of elements that inform and impact boundaries for ourselves and others in the world around us.

PART II

SEVEN

SAFETY IN A CULTURE OF FEAR

WE ARE ALL IMPACTED BY THE ENVIRONMENT WE LIVE, WORK, PLAY, LOVE, and set boundaries in. Our environment affects the way we think about safety, informs us of what we want and need, shapes personal perspective, and influences boundary setting. In this section, we will look at how mainstream cultural assumptions affect boundary setting, focusing in particular on how a culture of fear produces reactive approaches to safety. We will then explore ways to counter reactivity and develop alternatives.

THE BOX

When I taught classes at Home Alive, we developed an exercise called "The Box." It was adapted, in part, from a class activity introduced by Movements In Change, an amazing self-defense partnership formed in Portland, Oregon, in the 1990s. The adaptation I used began with the question, "What are the things each of you have been told will keep you safe?" I let people know they didn't have to like or agree with the things we were listing, they just had to be things they heard from friends, family, or via the news and media. While they brainstormed, I wrote their responses on a whiteboard. A typical list included:

- Act crazy
- Carry pepper spray
- Don't carry pepper spray, it will get used against you
- Make eye contact
- Don't make eye contact
- Don't look lost
- Be aware
- Lock your doors
- Don't walk alone
- Don't talk to strangers
- Stay in well-lit areas
- Don't go on dates with strangers
- Wear sensible shoes
- Carry a knife or other weapons
- Don't carry weapons, they can be used against you
- Be alert
- Don't go out alone
- Stay in groups
- Check doors before getting into your car or home
- Avoid "bad" parts of town
- Don't leave your drink unattended
- Don't drink or do drugs on the first date
- Walk with confidence
- Don't dress provocatively

After the brainstorm, I asked participants to reflect and notice what feelings, sensations, and thoughts surfaced from creating and observing this, and what the impact from making the list had on their bodies and their emotional state. People often shared feelings such as anger, fear, anxiety, hopelessness, and confusion. Sometimes someone would say that the list offered suggestions and options that felt empowering, but this was the rare exception. Mostly what people said they felt and what I observed in their body language and tone was fear. When participants asked what they should do in a particular situation or if something listed in The Box exercise really worked, I realized that even as we unpacked the problems with providing a one-size-fits-all checklist, that people still wanted (and expected) me to produce one.

We live in a world full of checklists, from popular magazine essays on "Five Steps to Self Confidence!" to academic articles outlining "Ten Things You Can Do to Impact Climate Change." We also live in a culture that propagates fear in a myriad of ways, including mainstream media news coverage that inflates a sense of danger, while simultaneously offering actionable step sounds bites and checklists to assuage the same fears they stoke. Author Barry Glassner calls this inflated sense of danger an American fear-ridden environment and argues that it is our perception of danger that has increased in the past few decades, not the actual level of risk. His book *The Culture of Fear: Why Americans Are Afraid of the Wrong Things* explores how our perceptions of fear are manipulated and magnified. There are hundreds of research studies and articles exploring how mainstream media exploits fear through an exaggerated focus on violence while simultaneously framing acts of compassion, kindness, and even self-defense as unique and exceptional. This approach prepares viewers for digestible and easily assimilated checklist "solutions" geared toward mitigating fear rather than changing conditions or exploring root causes of violence.

FEAR-BASED CHECKLISTS

In boundary-setting and self-defense classes I saw the impact of living in a culture of fear. Participants wanted definitive answers as to the right way to keep safe. Self-defense classes were seen as a place to get a safety checklist of dos and don'ts. However, this fear-based checklist approach as I came to call it, actually reinforces rather than diminishes a culture of fear, and blames victims in the process. When something bad happens, worry, fear, and anxiety prompt people try to find the reason it happened in order to avoid it in the future. This logic assumes that if one finds the reason for why something bad happened, then they can choose to do or not do whatever that was, and hence remain safe. This tactic soothes fears and offers a tangible action to prevent violence. It is human nature to approach safety this way. Our brains are wired to learn from our environments. If our ancestors witnessed someone eat berries, vomit, and then die, they would do well to not eat the same berries. This logic, however, when applied to current situations of violence, abuse, and interpersonal harm (as opposed to which plants to avoid eating), positions victims as responsible for what happened while reducing or even "invisiblizing" the accountability of those who chose to engage in violence or abuse.

While the intent behind trying to figure out the reason for a horrible event is to avoid it occurring again, the impact directs the blame toward victims/survivors. For example, when people offer assurances that it is never a woman's fault when she is sexually assaulted yet also try to figure out *what happened* in an attempt to avoid a similar situation, the focus typically falls on individual behaviors (and her actions primarily), thus creating the underlying message that what happened occurred because of something she did or did not do. This reasoning obscures the reality that the assault occurred because someone chose to assault. It is important to include perpetrators, boundary crossers, transgressors, bystanders, and witnesses in the framework from which we are exploring the context.

While there are clear-cut scenarios in which there is no question an assault has occurred, there are many instances that are much more complicated, which makes it even more important to develop the capacity to explore context and culpability from numerous perspectives. Sometimes boundary crossings are black and white: "I said no and you ignored it." But many are not so clear, as interpersonal interactions and the perspective(s) from which we are looking for "the cause" are informed by socialization, experience, communication style, upbringing, access to power, privilege, being a target of social or systemic oppression, culture, and personality, among other factors. I have witnessed this "search for the cause" play out in classes. A participant will share an incident involving some sort of harm—typically a mugging, an assault, harassment, or bullying— and class members then try to identify *why* it happened by asking for details. When they find something that seems like the cause or the triggering event, they discuss how to avoid similar situations in the future by "fixing" the identified "problem." In this way, class discussions often became brainstorming sessions about how to ensure a specific skill or technique will work in a particular scenario.

In discussing an incident, people's fear of that happening to them and surfacing emotions due to their own past experiences drive the conversation toward "solutions" to avoid rather than seeing what people did to survive a horrible incident. While trying to avoid violence and harm is understandable, and exploring options and choices can be empowering, the tone of these discussions demonstrates the powerful impact of a fear-based checklist approach to safety. In this paradigm, violence is a given and the best tactic is individual-focused (personal safety) with an undercurrent of victim blaming ("It's not your fault but here is what *you* need to do to avoid that happening in the future"). Rarely did discussions focus on what the person engaging in harmful behaviors could do to prevent incidents, or on ways to change larger social conditions that ignore and even encourage violence. Of course, people come to self-defense and boundary-setting classes to learn safety and interpersonal skills.

But I began to be deeply struck by how much a fear-based checklist framework narrows the way we approach the concept of well-being and safety.

In all the years I have facilitated The Box exercise, when I asked the question, "What are some things each of you have been told will keep you safe?" the answers almost exclusively place responsibility for safety on those surviving (or trying to avoid and prevent) violence and abuse. Answers like, "Don't rape someone … Don't abuse other people … Don't violate people … Don't beat people up … Hold your friends and community accountable for the things they do that create a climate where violence is more likely to happen … Create and nurture a support system … Build vibrant communities and reach out to those who try to isolate ourselves…" were not on the lists we created in class. The responses in class reflected how people are used to the concept of addressing violence as an individual issue and not a community concern; the depth to which we hold victims responsible; and how a culture of fear promotes a desire for quick-fix checklists.

I was also struck by how this framework rendered invisible or minimized the skillful actions people took. Another underlying assumption with the checklist approach is that "good" self-defense or boundary setting prevents something bad from happening. The reality is, however, that someone could use amazing skills and bad things can (and do) still happen. The desire to prevent violence and abuse is understandable. The fear-based checklist approach, however, creates a foundation that erodes a person's ability to recognize the skills they are already using and decreases self-trust. When people share a personal story and then ask themselves, *what should I have done?*, the assumption is that they either did not use any skills, or whatever skills they did use were not effective because something bad still happened (which is yet another way to victim blame). It became increasingly clear to me that I needed to create a new framework from which participants would learn new self-defense and boundary-setting skills.

REFRAMING THE SKILLS WE USE

After a class participant shared an incident and before brainstorming any options or ideas, I first asked people to identify all the self-defense and boundary-setting skills the person used in the situation. Often this was quite an emotional and excruciating process. Sometimes people would name something they did while undermining the skillfulness of it, reflecting the (false) assumption that had it been skillful they would have been able to stop what happened. It was important to use the process of naming and framing actions as self-defense and boundary setting as a way to interrupt victim blaming while also empowering people to see all the brilliant ways they were taking care of themselves and one another. Asking people to reframe their memory of a situation by seeing all the things they (or other people) *did do*, before discussing things they might want to try in the future, also functioned to reorient people's views of traumatic events by decreasing the pervasive sense of fear and helplessness, and interrupted the checklist assumption that there is a right way to prevent and survive violence.

One spring when I was teaching classes at Home Alive, local news ran a story about a number of young middle school girls who had survived an attempted assault by an unidentified man. It seemed he had tried to abduct a handful of girls who managed to get away. The story ran nightly for a few days, during which time the man attempted to abduct two more girls and assaulted another young girl, who was the only one who saw the man's face. She was able to work with a police sketch artist to identify him. The man was arrested later that day.

During this time, Home Alive received dozens of calls to set up classes in schools and youth programs. Worried parents called about our in-house class schedule and the news media made request after request for a story about how young girls can protect themselves. What struck me as I watched the story unfold was how nothing was mentioned about how all these girls had protected themselves. It seemed everyone only saw vulnerable, helpless young women. I saw something different. A large adult male made numerous attempts to abduct and assault adolescent girls who successfully fought him off. He was finally able to overpower one young girl who had survived the assault, got away, and within hours was working with the police, who were then able to identify and arrest him. This, in my mind, was not a community of helpless young girls but a group of badass middle-schoolers who deserved some light to be shined on the skillful way they handled themselves. It turns out they kicked at his knees and shins (target points), screamed, yelled for help, stomped on his feet, sought out support, walked in groups, told the man to go away, and ran away. The young girl who was sexually assaulted fought her attacker during the entire assault, got away from him with her arms and legs duct taped, ran and got help, and then had the emotional, mental, and physical capacity to work with the police. All of these are examples of self-defense and boundary-setting skills. It is important to not lose sight of the ways all of us are doing the best we can to navigate sometimes very terrifying and harrowing situations.

FEAR AND THE REACTIVE MINDSET

Why would statements like "Teach our friends and family to take care of one another" and "Don't abuse people" not be items that get put on The Box list? Fear. Fear permeates the American landscape. Media heighten our fear of danger with every alarming news story. Daily coverage of crimes, violence, potential terrorist threats, school shootings, poisonous drinking water, food insecurity, toxic toys, and stories of interpersonal violence cultivate a fear of our environment and one another. Fear generates anxiety, reactivity, and an impulse to seek quick, reductive answers. In a climate of fear, it feels better to have a safety checklist. A safety checklist seems like a guarantee. And while there might be some acknowledgement that there are no true guarantees in life, it feels better to have one just in case. When something happens to someone on the news or to someone we know, we can refer to the checklist and feel a sense of relief: *Phew, what a horrible thing, but it's not likely to happen to me because I do X or don't do Y.* This not only blames survivors, it also redirects the responsibility from perpetrators to those same survivors, and it isolates us from each other at the very times we need support and community.

The fear-based checklist also assumes violence to be a given. While it is true that we unfortunately live in a world where violence happens all too often, the checklist stops us from envisioning a world where violence is less likely to happen. It reduces self-defense to a reactive mode, which, at its core, reflects a belief that while we may be empowered to stop violence in the immediate moment, we are powerless to change the larger context of violence. Self-defense and boundary setting should include not just tools for responding to and preventing violence in the moment but also skills we can use to envision and create relationships, environments, and social constructs where safety is not a privilege but a basic right; where violence is less likely to occur; and where, if it does occur, we have the means to respond and hold each other accountable without simply "pathologizing" (i.e., regarding and treating someone as aberrant or abnormal), criminalizing, or victim blaming. There are many amazing groups and organizations exploring the intersections between individual and community self-defense, self-determination, and social transformation in a variety of creative and inspiring ways. The Box exercise provides a way to widen and contextualize concepts of self-defense in order to create a different, more flexible, and complex framework from which class participants learn specific physical skills. A few articles and organizations contextualizing the intersections between self-defense and social transformation include:

- "Understanding Self-Defense in the Civil Rights Movement Through Visual Arts" by Sonia James-Wilson (www.civilrights -teaching.org/Handouts/UnderstandingSelf-Defense.pdf)

- "Kicking Down The Barriers: Self-Defense and Social Change" by Martha Thompson (http://www.strategicliving.org/downloads /KiaiKickingDown.pdf)

- "Who Is Oakland: Anti-Oppression Activism, the Politics of Safety, and State Co-optation" by Ludmilap (CROATOAN) (http://escalatingidentity.wordpress.com/2012/04/30/who-is-oakland-anti-oppression-politics-decolonization-and-the-state/)

- "Resisting Gender Violence Without Cops or Prisons: An Interview with Victoria Law" by Angola 3 News (http://www.truth-out.org/news/item/5436:resisting-gender-violence-without-cops-or-prisons-an-interview-with-victoria-law)

- Incite! (http://www.incite-national.org/)

UNPACKING THE BOX

Most things that people included in The Box exercise were stranger focused. Stranger-oriented safety strategies do not necessarily reflect the violence people are likely to face because many assaults occur between people who know one another. Knowing the person who is causing you harm complicates self-care, boundary-setting, and self-defense strategies in ways that are important to include in any self-defense curriculums. The Box exercise is a way to begin to widen and deepen discussions about safety, violence, and self-defense. The options included in The Box were presented in a decontextualized way that perpetuated the myth that there is a right and wrong way to respond in various situations. This renders invisible the complexities that inform how people choose to defend themselves, stigmatizes certain choices, and can encourage victim blaming.

After seeing the list of safety tips in The Box exercise, we discussed as a class how the list reflects myths and perceptions about violence and offers a particular view of what violence is. For example, many items addressed interpersonal or one-on-one violence rather than social systems of violence. The strategies often assume access to doors that can be locked and that safety lies behind locked doors. Strategies such as "act crazy" are not only demeaning, they ignore the reality of institutional violence and the vulnerability of individuals identified as mentally ill. Self-defense tactics like "stay out of certain neighborhoods" have very different meanings depending on who you are in the world. For people of color in general, and black men in particular, who are often viewed as dangerous and/or criminal, being more vigilant and aware in certain environments is a very important self-defense strategy. On the other hand, saying, "Stay out of certain neighborhoods" can also reflect complex and intersecting myths about class and race that stigmatize certain neighborhoods based on stereotypes. Most of the options included in The Box exercise focus on individual safety and individual acts of violence, which can limit critical thinking about systems of violence and delimit safety strategies to individualistic approaches where violence is viewed as inevitable.

GIVING UP THE CHECKLIST

Let me be clear: the action steps listed in The Box exercise are not wrong, and some of them will be the best choice for different people in different contexts. I am encouraging us to exchange the checklist and a one-size-fits-all approach to safety for self-trust and belief in our own ability to do the best we can in any given moment. Not only can we respond to, and at times prevent, violence and abuse, but we can even survive and thrive in spite of it. This can be scary. Inevitably, in self-defense classes someone will share a story that in their mind represents a boundary-gone-bad or no-boundary-at-all scenario and asks, "What should I do?" In the dynamic of "teacher as expert," I am expected to answer the "should" as a means to offer some kind of guarantee of safety: You should do X, then Y will be avoided, and Z will not happen. The problem with answering this question within a checklist framework is that it does not consider the context in very deep or meaningful ways.

Another problem is the "What if's?" themselves. "What if's?" are a never-ending series of possibilities: *What if* you do X and then

Y happens? *What if* you try A and it doesn't work? *What if* you set a boundary and they don't listen? *What* if you use (fill in a boundary-setting or self-defense skill here) and the person gets angry? *What if* there is more than one person bullying you? *What if* you lose your nerve? *What if* you forget how to get out of a choke hold? "What if's" reproduce fear, anxiety, and self-doubt, in part because they are never ending and because they seek certainty where there is none. They are an understandable product of living in a culture of fear that offers a checklist-oriented approach to safety, but they are ultimately ineffective as a general approach. With the goal of encouraging people to trust their capacity to assess a situation and make informed decisions on what to do based on their own expertise rather than on a checklist, Home Alive teachers developed an exercise called "What's Free? What's Open?" This exercise involves taking the particulars of a given scenario and asking what is available, accessible, possible, realistic, and (hopefully) effective to meet your goals. In a self-defense situation, this may mean looking for what target points are vulnerable and available in a particular moment and what tools, weapons, and shields you have at your disposal. What's Free? What's Open? can also be used to look at events that have happened as a way to identify the skills people utilized but did not recognize as self-defense or boundary setting.

Negotiating boundaries and safety means having a critical understanding of context that informs when and how one might set boundaries and even what safety might look like. What's Free? What's Open? will look very different due to different situations for different people. The goal of using What's Free? What's Open? is to think about what resources, skills, and capacity you have, what information you know about the other person and situation, and what your sense is about the best way to approach and obtain your goal. What's Free? What's Open? is not a way to create a new series of checklists; rather it is a way to reframe how we approach scary, uncomfortable, intimidating, or frightening situations by encouraging curious reflection on the complexity of context and the variability of how people can and do respond.

It can be challenging to move away from a formulaic approach, especially when fear motivates us to seek standardized strategies. People, however, are not arithmetic problems. We're not even the wordy math question you get on the SAT. Imagine the following scenario …

Martha, starting at 8:00 a.m., felt her intuition kick in because the person talking to her at the café began to ask very personal questions in what she perceived to be a pushy and inappropriately flirty way that made her feel uncomfortable. She began to deflect these questions and set boundaries at 8:07 a.m. by saying, "You know, I'm not really comfortable sharing that information with you." In such a case, how long is the anticipated time before the person Martha is talking to responds to her boundaries, and what is the anticipated response?

A. The person backs off within three seconds.

B. No time. The person is unaware that a boundary has been set.

C. No time. The person ignores Martha's boundary, using humor and minimization: "Come on, it's no big deal."

D. After ten seconds of reflection, the person apologizes and respects Martha's boundary.

What should Martha do? People ask this kind of question all the time and in classes, as in life, people are overflowing with advice, ideas, and opinions about exactly what Martha should do: "She should leave … She should tell the person she thinks it's rude to ask personal questions … She should ask them personal questions back … She should start picking her nose and freak the person out … Tell the person she has to go to the bathroom and ignore them when she gets out … Pretend she sees someone she knows or just remembered she has a meeting and has to go…" The truth is that none of these things are what Martha should do. Yet any of these could be possibilities. First, we don't have a lot of information about the context or who this person is. A stranger? A coworker? A longtime friend? Partner? Ex-partner? Date from last night? Someone she wants to go on a date with? Second, we don't have any information about what Martha would like to have happen. All we know is that she is uncomfortable. Is she uncomfortable because she would like to be able to talk about these things with this person but isn't sure how? Or uncomfortable because she wants to say something but hates conflict? Is she anxious because she feels threatened? Or is she anxious because she doesn't want to share personal information? All of these things inform boundaries. There is no right way to respond and there is no response that will guarantee a specific reaction from someone.

In one class, during a "What if?" discussion, someone asked what you should do if a perpetrator gets you in a car to take you to a second location. The room was full of fear and desperation. No one said a word until I directed the discussion to an exploration of context. Then two participants finally spoke up. One was a young man who had disclosed some information about what was understood to be a long history of very violent trauma. He quietly said something to the effect of, "I would do whatever it took to not get in the car. I don't care what happens. I won't ever let something like that happen to me again." The other participant, a middle-aged woman, said something very different: "I would do whatever I needed to live. I can't imagine my baby girl growing up without me." Two very different self-defense strategies, and in fact two different views on what self-defense would look like, and a clear example of how there is no one right way to act in any given situation.

Fear and anxiety drive us to offer advice and suggestions to others about what to do. This reflects an attempt to fix the situation rather than cultivate a wider awareness of what is going on both internally and externally. Advice is often a vehicle through which people project their perspectives, morals, and beliefs onto a situation in a generalizing way. Anytime someone says, "You should ..." they are projecting a belief about the right way to handle a situation, which may or may not be the best (or even possible) way for someone else. When advice is informed by a sense of intuition, it can be challenging to comprehend that one person's intuition can be very different from someone else's. But it can be and often times is. When we mistake our intuition for "the objective truth" we often miss important information. We don't necessarily have to explain or defend or justify our intuition, but we should be able to identify what it's based on.

What we observe, how we think about safety, the kinds of boundaries we want, how we build our support systems, which action items from The Box exercise we find to be useful, are all informed by our environment and who we are in the world. Fear can narrow our perspective, which at times is a good thing. We don't need to spend time reflecting on context when we are about to get hit by a bus. Other times, it can be helpful to widen our view of things, be curious and reflective. Moving toward a more reflective and responsive way of setting and negotiating boundaries can be challenging in the face of strong emotions like fear, anger, and anxiety. In the next chapter, we will look at some tools to help navigate the complicated conditions in which boundaries are set or negotiated, and how to do so with a framework that allows for the full range of human emotions and experiences.

EIGHT

SETTING BOUNDARIES WITH INTENTION

BOUNDARIES CAN BE MESSY. NOT ONLY DO THEY INVOLVE BOUNDARY setting itself, but boundaries are also set in emotional, interpersonal, psychological, and physical contexts that impact us. There are times when we cross people's boundaries without knowing, set boundaries in ways that are hurtful to people we don't want to hurt, are hurt by other people's boundaries, set a boundary we later regret, or don't set a boundary we wish we had. The collateral effects of setting and negotiating a boundary are often enormous and complicated.

This chapter considers how the concepts of compassion, forgiveness, accountability, community outreach, and solidarity can help us grapple with the messy and complicated world of boundary setting. Some of these concepts are drawn from current psychology, some from spiritual traditions, and some from contemporary political organizing (including the transformative justice movement). Some may be familiar to you and some may be new. All are offered here as means of understanding boundary work in a larger setting. Setting boundaries with intention is another way of understanding how the personal can be political and how individual work can contribute to positive shifts in society. For more information on transformative justice, go to www.transformativejustice.eu/en/.

Forgiveness and Compassion

Forgiveness is an important skill and not something to rush into or engage in before we are ready and willing. Forgiveness, as I define it in this book, is not meant to be automatic or unearned. It is a process, often to be taken slowly and with intention. Reflecting on forgiveness frequently means stepping back and investigating events with curiosity and as much compassion as we can muster, in order to understand what happened in a nonjudgmental way. The goal and end result of reflecting on and seeking understanding may not necessarily always be to forgive. In addition, while the goal of initial exploration is to try to understand without rushing to judge, making judgments themselves is not to be avoided completely. There will be events, interactions, and behaviors that warrant judgment (both good and bad). The intention of this practice is to not rush to judgment while being mindful and accountable when we do judge.

Contemplating what conditions make forgiveness possible can be valuable. Primarily because when we mess up, make mistakes, hurt people, get hurt, set boundaries out of guilt, anger, or resentment, lose sight of our intentions and values, react defensively, and are in many other ways exquisitely human, it benefits us to be able to be compassionate in our reflection. Forgiveness, at its core, is an act of compassion, both self-directed and outward or other-directed. The aim is not to always be compassionate and forgive everyone, but to be able to choose to reflect on events with a compassionate lens that extends the possibility of forgiveness if conditions allow. It also invites people to investigate what conditions are necessary for forgiveness, which can help create avenues for accountability. Again, this is not to suggest that the purpose of accountability is forgiveness. There may be times when we do not want to or are unable to extend compassion and forgiveness. This is understandable in some situations. A survivor of domestic violence may find that not extending compassion toward her or his abuser is a healing position to take. Someone who was cruelly bullied may not want to forgive his or her attackers. I have many clients who have made very thoughtful and grounded decisions to not forgive certain people. The important aspect is developing the capacity to have an intentional compassionate lens, so that any decision made to not extend compassion or forgiveness is an active, intentional choice.

DEVELOPING COMPASSIONATE CURIOSITY

Clients and class participants have shared that talking about compassion and forgiveness makes them feel as if they are being asked to not be angry or hurt. While this is an understandable reaction, I believe the contrary—that compassion enables people to feel *more*, not less. Having compassion increases one's capacity to be present to the full range of human emotions and experiences, which include feelings that are not typically associated with compassion, such as rage, anger, or bitterness. As a first step, rather than tell ourselves we must forgive or be compassionate, we might find that learning to develop some curiosity about our situation can help with understanding it. The ability to reflect on events to seek clarity and understanding without preemptively judging offers us more information than when we make reactive snap judgments or find ourselves reenacting old scenarios in habitual ways.

Snap judgments are typically rapid assessments of people, events, and situations. A client shared an example of his awareness of making a snap judgment, which, in this case, also helped him understand where the judgment originated. He realized that he assumed his coworker would be resentful if he left early, and in anticipating her reaction, he became preemptively defensive. When she was not resentful in reality but rather both understanding and accepting, my client realized he made a snap judgment based on how her mannerisms reminded him of an ex-girlfriend.

An example of cultivating awareness for habitual or adaptive patterns comes from another client. Together we explored new ways she could navigate her relationship with her mother, which held a complex set of patterns and reactions. My client explained that she felt as if she were a handball being whacked around by her mother and her mother's emotions whenever they interacted, and she was having difficulty understanding what was happening in the interactions that made her feel this way. We decided to approach our exploration using both curiosity and compassion. This process involved examining an interaction and exploring the answers to the following questions (without judgment):

- ◆ What happened? A moment-to-moment look at events as they unfold—like watching a play and stating what each performer is doing and saying scene-by-scene.

- ◆ What was my experience (including thoughts, sensations, and feelings) during each "freeze frame" moment?

- ◆ What was my perspective of the other person's experience?

- ◆ What did I want and need in those moments?

- ◆ What context was this happening in (including external events, time, and place)?

- ◆ How was I impacted? How was the other person impacted?

- ◆ What am I feeling in this moment as I recall what happened?

- ◆ What do I currently want as I recall what happened?

- ◆ How do I feel about this want/need?

By exploring questions like these, my client came to the decision to discontinue contact with her mother without being consumed with guilt or defensiveness about her needs and boundaries. She was, in fact, able to feel an intense range of feelings about her relationship with her mother more acutely as a result of viewing the events with compassionate curiosity. This allowed her to tend to her guilt, anger, and pain in new ways that promoted her own healing.

Clients have also let me know that focusing on self-compassion and forgiveness feels like they are letting themselves off the hook for harmful things they have done. Forgiving themselves, they inform me, would minimize the damage of what they did and diminish the punishment they deserve. Compassion and forgiveness do not in any way equate to not being accountable; they are not a means to avoid feeling the guilt and pain of having caused harm. Self-directed compassion and reflecting on forgiveness (without rushing the process) actually help people experience feelings more intensely, not less, and this aids in making decisions about how to address the harm that has occurred.

A client who was struggling with the concept of compassion and reflecting on forgiveness when thinking about the damage he had caused in his relationship told me about his "light bulb moment." He came to session one day and shared that once he was finally able to be a little compassionate with himself about having engaged in behaviors that made his partner feel threatened and afraid, he was able to really listen to her. When she talked about feeling frightened and the pain that it caused her, he didn't "crumple up in a big guilt ball," as he put it. In other words, his capacity to be self-compassionate actually allowed him to be more present to the pain he caused, which made it easier for him to validate her experience and be held accountable.

REVENGE AND ACCOUNTABILITY

Guilt, fear, and helplessness are distressing emotions. Sometimes anger, resentment, and desire for revenge feel more powerful. Revenge, like the checklists from the previous chapter discussed, is an understandable reaction to intense and painful feelings and is an attempt to mitigate fear and helplessness. The problem is that revenge does not reduce fear or distress and actually prolongs suffering, because it circumvents our capacity to feel the pain necessary to heal. While it is normal for some people to feel vengeful after an incident of harm or abuse, getting stuck in those feelings makes people less resilient and fuels a culture of fear. Wanting revenge is not the same as seeking accountability. Revenge is the desire to inflict hurt because you have been hurt. There will be situations in which it will be appropriate for someone to inflict pain as result of being hurt. Punching back when someone hits you may be the best choice in a given situation. Countering a hurtful comment with a witty retort that stings can also be effective. Asking someone to imagine your pain by recalling hurtful times in his or her own life can be a powerful way to evoke empathy. The intent is to increase available strategies across situations rather than demarcate choices by getting mired in revenge or stuck in feeling angry. Compassionate curiosity broadens possibilities without precluding emotions, negative or positive, by not judging them preemptively.

Let's say Maria's supervisor sexually harassed her. She is angry that her supervisor, an older white man with a lot of privilege, a lot of money, and a lot of stinky cologne, did this. She is pissed that she didn't respond the way she imagined she would and is upset that he got away with it, that he is still the supervisor, and because he has the resources, will likely remain so. She is conflicted about whether or not to fight him in court and has quit her job to look for other work. She is aware that this was her decision, but she is angry at her boss and hates him for making her have to make this choice. Not cool. Maria is aware that she is angry with men right now, and with white rich men with stinky cologne in particular. She can no longer be touched in certain ways and is having somatic reactions when people approach her, including flinching, anxiety, tensing up, and feelings of panic and rage. At first, her anger propels her to action, which feels good, positive, and empowering. Then she realizes the boundaries she initially set out of anger are no longer serving her. She no longer wants to automatically yank away from any touch by a man, be it a friend, coworker, peer, or family member, and put up an angry, defensive wall. The hope is that Maria could be gentle and forgiving with herself for having been angry and needing to put up walls; she would hope that her male friends, peers, coworkers, and family members could understand and forgive her defenses, rather than take her boundaries personally, and find compassionate ways to engage with her. Maria hopes that any hurt her friends or family are feeling can be handled with compassion no matter what her boundaries were, and that they can remain compassionate throughout the process as Maria navigates through and changes them. Compassion and reflecting on the possibility of forgiveness soften the healing process and allow boundaries to be different at different times with different people. They allow accountability for the impact of a boundary to be upheld within the complexity of why the boundary may have been necessary.

SHAME AND GUILT

When we talk about responsibility, accountability, and forgiveness, we must distinguish between our behaviors and ourselves, and between shame and guilt. There are important psychological, cognitive, and experiential differences between guilt and shame. The experience of shame is about the self, who we are as a person, the deepest part of who we believe we are. Shame encompasses our self-awareness and wraps the self in negative self-consciousness. There is evidence that the experience of shame involves more somatic sensations than experiences of guilt. That is, we seem to feel shame more in our bodies, internally, because the sense of shame is about us. The experience of guilt, in contrast, is less (even if only slightly) of a somatic experience and contains critique and negative evaluation in connection with a behavior, an action, or event—something *outside* the self. There are cognitive differences as well:

> *Those experiencing shame tended to see themselves as worthless and powerless—unable to make changes in the environment or themselves. By contrast, those experiencing guilt saw themselves as able to take some sort of corrective action either towards the consequences of their behavior or toward future behavior .... In shame, the source of blame or negative valuation of the self was localized as "out there" originating in the "other." This externalizing of blame was one of the chief markers of shame. Even as an internal experience, shame involved judgment of an internalized disapproving other. With guilt, by contrast, the internal evaluation system was felt to originate more from within a person's own sense of self.*[9]

---

[9] Parker, Stephen, and Rebecca Thomas. "Psychological Differences in Shame vs. Guilt: Implications for Mental Health Counselors." *Journal of Mental Health Counseling*, Vol 31(3), July 2009: 213-24.

The experience of shame signals that there is something irreparably wrong with the self, and it causes people to either blame themselves with a sense of hopelessness, or shift the blame onto others, neither of which create space for repair, taking responsibility, accountability, or forgiveness. Shame involves a withdrawal from people, experiences, and incidents either by lashing out or turning inward; guilt motivates attempts to repair, which, even if unimaginable to achieve, remains a significant possibility. It is important to distinguish between guilt and shame. If someone is experiencing shame, there may be work to be done to strengthen the ego-self or internal self before moving on to exploring forgiveness and accountability. If someone is experiencing guilt and repair seems possible, they may already have the emotional resiliency to move toward taking responsibility and being accountable. Sometimes the experience of guilt can be overwhelming and incapacitating, making repair a tiny and distant hope on a very bleak horizon. In this case, as in the case of experiencing shame, before moving toward accountability, work may need to be done in first strengthening the core self, increasing self-confidence, and developing self-directed kindness and empathy (which are achieved through compassionate curiosity).

ACCOUNTABILITY AND RESPONSIBILITY

According to our dear friend Webster, the word "accountable" means being subject to explain one's actions, inactions, choices, behaviors, or decisions. "Responsibility," according to our same friend, includes blame, blameworthiness, being at fault or guilty. Assigning responsibility implies seeking out who or what to blame, while accountability seeks to understand what happened and why in order to construct a framework for responsibility. Taking responsibility is a component of accountability, one that comes after the challenging work of developing a comprehensive understanding of the situation. This takes time, energy, and commitment and can feel uncomfortably slow in our current fast-paced, reactive culture. Responsibility is often positioned as something to be assigned immediately so that things can be fixed and everyone can move on. This is how we have been taught to think about forgiveness as well. We ask for forgiveness, we get it, and things go back to normal. Forgiveness in this context relies solely on responsibility and not on accountability: You take responsibility for your actions, then seek and hopefully receive forgiveness. If you do not receive forgiveness, well, you did what you could. This approach tends to be individual-focused and is designed to make someone feel better while restoring the relationship. It does not typically address the conditions under which the incident occurred or how to change those conditions to prevent it from happening in the future. Accountability, even when focused on what one person can do to address the harm they have caused, involves the painful process of examining what happened, exploring the complexity of why, and seeking to understand the complicated and social conditions in which the event(s) occurred, all while grappling with questions about what is necessary in order for someone to take responsibility. A great place to begin your exploration of accountability and to learn how to start on the accountability process is by contacting a local Transformative Justice Project.

Given the choice between turning to face the pain—to move through it and find peace within the storm—and finding a quick fix, we often choose the latter. The former seems more complicated. And indeed it most often is. Accountability asks that people sit with, or really feel and grapple with, the painful reality of what occurred and makes visible the conditions in which it happened. This is challenging and made even more so when we do not have the skills, tools, capacity, or the role models needed for engaging in the process. A punitive approach to harm that does not involve the hard work of addressing conditions; the complicated factors that inform the context; and the difficult work of imaging what accountability and repair might look like can, at times, end up being more harmful than helpful. If someone crosses a boundary and is punished for it but left with no understanding of what happened or why, not only is repair limited, but the conditions under which the boundary was crossed remain unexamined.

Taking responsibility means being capable of realizing what you are at fault for and at which point you are the one to blame. Accountability goes a step further and answers the following questions:

- What happened and why?
- What conditions are necessary to take responsibility?
- What would that look like?
- Is forgiveness possible? Why or why not?
- What does the person harmed need and want to have happen?
- Is that possible and if not, what steps can be taken?
- Are there conditions, social, systemic, interpersonal, and historical, that contributed to or allowed the harm to happen that need to be understood, addressed or changed?
- Are there community members, witnesses, bystanders, support systems, social systems that are important to consider or include in the process of accountability?

When we take responsibility within the context of accountability, the conditions required for healing, transformation, and resiliency are more possible. The road to accountability can seem long in a world of quick fixes and punitive reactions, but the journey itself is part of the process.

CHANGING BOUNDARIES, CHANGING SOCIETY

Traditionally, approaches to boundary setting focus on individual boundaries, primarily between two people. For example, saying no to an unwanted request, or asking a friend to be supportive in a particular way. While important, this is only one aspect of boundaries. Negotiating wants and needs is also social as well as interpersonal, and boundaries are an important part of building, nurturing, sustaining, and changing the community. Safety, self-defense and boundary setting are not just individual issues; they are community and social concerns, too. Standing up to a sexist, homophobic, and/or racist manager may involve setting a boundary with them. It can also be a way to change workplace protocol, interrupt a culture of silence, bring to light systems of oppression, and even act as a catalyst for labor organizing, engaging community members, and creating local social transformation. While it is not critical that you always consider the social conditions in which boundaries are being set, context is important.

Home Alive, the organization whose methods inform much of this book, was originally established in 1993 by a group of Seattle artists and musicians in response to the many forms of violence, abuse, and harm our community was grappling with, including the horrifying rape and murder of Mia Zapata. Because Home Alive was founded and supported by so many artists and musicians, we organized events in clubs and bars on a regular basis. These events included art, music, speakers, and information booths. I was often asked to speak at these shows, and over time I noticed that the culture in the venues was shifting in response to community dialogues that occurred naturally because of and in response to the events. I overheard men who were in no way political and would never identify as an activist or feminist talk about how to respond to friends who are emotionally or physical abusive to their girlfriends. Bartenders pulled money for cab fare at the end of the night so that no one had to walk home alone. There was a shift in thinking about how people can take care of one another and keep each other safe that was a direct response to community conversations about self-care, self-defense, and boundary setting. The shift was by no means perfect, but it reflected a spirit of solidarity that allowed people who would not otherwise participate in any formal community organizing or anti-violence work to engage in a form of social change.

Home Alive events encouraged people to consider safety a community issue while supporting a wide range of self- and community-directed responses: bands asked for information to hand out on tours; artists organized shows; writers wrote and performed; audience members collected cab fare for people or organized systems for rides home; bartenders gave out referrals to domestic violence shelters and asked us to provide informal trainings for staff on responding to inter-personal violence; Mothers Against Police Brutality educated us about the historical roots of self-defense in the black community and about how Home Alive could support their work; drag queens doing late night patrols on Seattle's Capitol Hill to stop gay bashings asked for trainings—and trained us on teaching self-defense skills in high heels; activists organized workshops on understanding consent and account-ability for people who have crossed boundaries; anarchists made zines; tech workers organized booths at job fairs; women in the sex industry coordinated classes designed for and by them; queer youth clubs ran panels on bullying and self-defense.

At Home Alive, I worked to support these various events that encour-aged critical dialogue about community safety, self-defense, and how to support radically different groups and communities whose approach to and even concept of safety and self-defense were different at different times based on social context. What are the connections and avenues for solidarity between a rock band asking audience members to support local self-defense classes, a homeless youth group hosting workshops to address sexual assault in their community, artists organizing a benefit auction to raise awareness of domestic violence, and a round table on police brutality? For me, working at Home Alive, it was important to build bridges between the various ways communities approached safety, boundary setting and self-defense in order to increase social solidarity and community support directed at changing the multitude of condi-tions in which violence occurs. To me, this was a reflection of the com-plexity of claiming that self-defense is a community issue because safety and self-defense are important to different communities in different ways. Self-defense became a conduit for cultivating a sense of solidarity.

SOLIDARITY

Solidarity is a defined as, among other things, a "union or fellowship arising from common responsibilities and interests." Negotiating safety and boundaries is not just about setting a limit, asking for a need to be met, or saying no to an unwanted request. Negotiating boundaries is a way of relating to other people and to the world we live in. While there will be times when we do not care about the impact our boundaries have on others, there will be situations where we will care a lot. Setting boundaries with a larger spirit of solidarity means developing a broad sense of how your actions are informed by and impact others within a social context. Social context considers current situations with an understanding and awareness of historical implications. This may mean developing an understanding of your partner's personal experience in regard to the challenges they have in saying no to unwanted requests and locating that understanding in the larger social context of who they are in the world.

Considering the consequences of our boundaries, being accountable and responsible are powerful when done with a sense of solidarity. Accountability by its very nature asks us to actively listen to the person who has been harmed, seek to understand their experiences, and to the best of our ability, offer the reparation they request. When amends are made or people engage in restitution for harm with an appreciation of common interests, it becomes easier to imagine more possibilities of how to be in the world, how to create conditions in which harm is less likely to occur, and how to address it collectively when it does happen. It also allows us to see how much we gain when being accountable, how accountability contributes to our own growth as well as to stronger and more resilient relationships and communities.

Solidarity asks us to attempt to hold onto people even when they have caused harm. This is counter to the mainstream punitive models that diagnose, pathologize, and criminalize perpetrators—all approaches that situate people outside the mainstream or "normal" society. Setting boundaries with a spirit of solidarity does not mean ignoring or enduring harm, nor does it require people to stay connected to or in community with someone who is dangerous or engaging in violence or abuse. It does ask that we use the skills of compassion and accountability to find ways to address incidents of violence and abuse that do not dehumanize. We are all capable of doing harm. We all have and will cross other people's boundaries. The extent to which we do matters tremendously. Ignoring a friend's statement that they do not want to go with you to a barbeque and showing up at their house because you are sure you will change their mind is very different than forcing someone into a sexual act against their will. These are extreme examples on opposite ends of the continuum of boundary crossing. But in between them are a great many scenarios that are gray and confusing with complex interpersonal and social contexts. Having an understanding of the complexity moves us away from black and white, right and wrong checklist thinking and creates a much richer blueprint for boundary work.

The mainstream culture of fear propels us toward an individualistic model of self-care. It is not bad to focus on oneself, but without a sense of solidarity we risk perpetuating the isolating, victim-blaming paradigms that in actuality make us less safe and make negotiating boundaries more difficult. Having a sense of solidarity invites us to connect our well-being to that of others, which in turn widens the possibilities for how to identify and negotiate needs, and encourages creative and compassionate approaches to boundary setting and self-care.

Boundaries are highly personal and interpersonal. We set them in social contexts imbued with history, culture, community, and individual experience(s) that inform various aspects of how, when, and why we set (or don't) set boundaries. Compassionate curiosity, forgiveness, accountability, responsibility, and a sense of solidarity suffuse boundary work with a practical dexterity that helps navigate the sometimes very clear and often very complicated work of negotiating and setting boundaries.

NINE

CREATING AND UNDERSTANDING SUPPORTS FOR BOUNDARY SETTING

BOUNDARIES ARE SET, NEGOTIATED, AND DEFENDED WITHIN RELA-tionships, social systems, and community. In order to set effective boundaries it's helpful to understand how you can build and nurture support systems for yourself. In relationships, giving and receiving support is key, but there are also interpersonal patterns and traps that can make it difficult to communicate.

Boundary setting involves learning from "mistakes," renegotiating limits (in some circumstances) as new or unexpected developments occur, and changing (or defending) boundaries when necessary in response to how they are received. The REFLECTIVE LOOP, discussed in chapter four, is helpful for all of these. Using this tool, which involves receiving and offering support, care, validation, and critical feedback, requires a social support system. If you don't already have a support system, you will need to build one. If you already have one, it may need tending to or nurturing. If you have a robust and healthy support system, great! No matter what kind of support system you have, it is important to consider that using the REFLECTIVE LOOP may be a new and very different way of interacting and relating to people.

CREATING A SUPPORT SYSTEM

Creating a support system can be an intimidating prospect for some people. It may be useful to view building one as a series of small steps, rather than as one large action item. First, make a list of everyone you know who you believe could offer validation, feedback, support, and/or constructive criticism. Some people may be able to offer all of these while others may be better at one or two. Can't think of anyone to put on your list? Make a list of activities that you can participate in where you will meet and establish connections with people who might someday be on the list. No idea how to get involved in activities? Here's a short list to get you started ...

- Volunteer with a group or program that shares your values/interests
- Host a dinner party with a "get to know one another better" theme
- Ask your friends, coworkers, or peers to throw a dinner party
- Connect with your faith community
- Go to all the social events you can and make an effort to introduce yourself and talk with different people
- Join (or start) a group, club, or class
- Participate in team events/sports
- Engage in social activities you enjoy with other people
- Let one or two people know you are reading this book and ask them to be part of creating your support system
- Start a reading group or book club with the theme of creating support systems
- Join a book club

If you are overwhelmed or it seems impossible to participate in activities and meet people, it may be helpful to address barriers and issues that are getting in the way. This could involve talking to a counselor, mentor, coach, spiritual guide, teacher, pastor, or priest or doing somatic practices, art therapy, writing, or other healing work.

NURTURING A SUPPORT SYSTEM

If you already have a great network of friends, family, and/or peers, your support system may still need some interpersonal maintenance. Many people with vibrant social networks report feeling lonely, disconnected, and isolated and lack support and feedback. Some people find it hard to ask for help no matter how many loving friends they have. Others may find it challenging to give advice or offer constructive feedback to people close to them. Sometimes people don't have skill or experience in providing validation, reflection, or critical feedback. Using the REFLECTIVE LOOP with friends and family may involve practicing unfamiliar skills, connecting with people in different ways, and forming new types of relationships.

Variety is healthy for human beings, from diet to exercise and relationships. Having a dynamic and robust support system means developing different kinds of relationships that meet different needs—not trying to have one or two people fill all your support roles. There are people who are better at offering compassion, but not so good at direct critical feedback and people who have the personality and skill to say it like it is, while others are much better at diplomacy. Tending to friendships allows them to grow, deepen, and mature, which can radically change interpersonal dynamics. Ultimately, tending to relationships in this way is about supporting people in being who they are, not trying to change them or their personalities.

USING THE REFLECTIVE LOOP

The REFLECTIVE LOOP is a practice of exploring, reflecting, and receiving feedback on intuition, self-care, and boundaries. The loop involves the flow of communication. That might mean giving yourself a chance to reflect on your own actions. It might mean a chance to reflect on and receive feedback from your various support systems. Using the loop can help you get "reality checks" on your motivation for setting a boundary, the effect and impact of setting it, and your desired outcome. Such a process can also help you gauge your emotional responses and safety needs, and social and cultural considerations. Reality checks are compassionate observations about a situation, interaction, or event that are free from interpretation, meaning-making, and judgment. Interpretations, meaning-making, and judgments are not inherently wrong, but this process encourages you to be able to look at events from somewhat of a distance. It is as if you and your support system are watching a play. First, you want to state what is happening and have everyone observe "the play" before offering interpretations, opinions, advice, validation, or other reflections. It is important to set the scene before engaging in feedback. Being able to pause and assess a situation before jumping in and offering validation, support, advice, or any other feedback is an important skill and allows people to practice being more responsive and less reactionary.

THE ADVICE TRAP

Constructive criticism and feedback are different from advice. The practice of using a reflective loop involves non-shaming and nonjudgmental reflection, exploration, feedback, and constructive criticism *before* any advice is asked for or offered. This process is important because seeking advice is often a means to avoid reflecting on challenging, difficult, emotionally charged events or situations. Thinking *I messed up! What should I do?* takes one down a different path than *I messed up! I wonder what contributed to my actions? How do I feel about what happened? Are there other steps I may have taken? If so, what got in the way of me taking them? Was there a payoff or unintentional benefit to my choice/ behavior?* Using the REFLECTIVE LOOP helps explore with compassionate curiosity rather than seek "the right answer" and can lead to more meaningful insight and options for change. This process invites one to sit with and increase one's capacity to feel uncomfortable and sometimes distressing emotions that arise when one is looking critically at events. While challenging, learning to feel emotions without reacting allows people to be able to see more clearly what is actually happening, rather than letting the event be clouded by strong emotions.

Another aspect of advice is that it often contradicts itself from person to person and if people do not trust themselves, it is easy to be overwhelmed, confused, and sometimes incapacitated by trying to decide what to do when people are offering different and sometimes wildly contradictory advice. One interesting rabbit hole of the advice trap is that confusion that arises from contradictory advice can lead people to seek more advice in the hope of discovering "the right" advice. This process is external; searching for an answer from an outside source is not inherently bad or wrong, but over time and without a strong core sense of self or resilient ego, this searching can erode one's self-trust. In other words, the process of seeking advice can actually impair our ability to trust ourselves.

Learning to filter advice, take it in, weigh it, and reflect on it without reacting immediately to each new piece helps keep people grounded and able to take action from a responsive rather than reactive place. Doing this requires listening to ourselves, which not only means being able to trust ourselves but also requires a sense of self, a "core" if you will. Having a resilient sense of self and the capacity to listen to and trust ourselves can be impacted by overwhelming experiences, trauma, abuse, systems of inequity, internalized oppression, isolation, family dynamics, illness, and physical and environmental factors, to name a few. Self-care and healing work are important tools for self-trust. These can take a variety of forms including counseling; somatic practices; yoga; meditation; art; music; writing; joining or starting groups; connecting with a naturopath, psychiatrist, doctor, or medical professional; joining a gym; getting out in nature; starting new relationships or ending unhealthy ones; eating well; exercising; volunteering; engaging with community; connecting with your faith;

and exploring other activities that get you in touch with yourself. The more we are in touch with ourselves, the more we can take advice for what it is: one piece of information among many others that informs how we may choose to respond to an event, situation, or interaction.

THE AGREEMENT TRAP

People don't always have to understand (or agree with) a boundary to respect it. There are times when having agreements about a boundary or request will be important. For example, a friend of mine asked for time off during a busy season at her job. In this case, she was very invested in having her supervisor understand and agree with why she needed a few days off in order to have it approved.

The agreement trap happens when the boundary or request is viewed as conditional. We often believe that if someone doesn't agree with our request, we don't have a right to set the boundary. This can create a great deal of pressure to explain why a boundary or request is important and why refusing to agree with it is unreasonable. This approach tends to polarize discussions into right/wrong contexts and can lead to attempts to not only change someone's mind but to also change their values and personal views.

For example, a client struggled with her boyfriend, who refused to agree that being twenty minutes late to meet her was a problem. She tried to get him to understand that she thought it was rude and made her feel unimportant. He countered with examples of how he demonstrated her importance to him in many ways, and expressed that being late had nothing to do with her and that she should "lighten up" on this issue. Over time, the argument devolved into more personal territory with her claiming that he was disrespectful and him stating that she was uptight. Each person defended their position in the hope that if they could just get the other person to understand why their approach/belief was right, the problem would be solved and things would improve between them. They got stuck in an escalating agreement trap that resulted in neither person feeling heard and both feeling defensive and hurt.

It can often help to let go of trying to agree. A fairly straightforward "Let's agree to disagree" approach sounds simple enough, but it can be challenging. The core of this strategy is the acceptance that the difference is unresolvable and that it is causing an issue that needs to be tended to. The goal then becomes finding ways to negotiate the difference. This approach creates room for collaborative problem-solving; it asks people to handle moments when differences arise and cause problems in relationships in ways that are rooted in accepting the difference rather than trying to make it go away (e.g., by trying to get the other person to agree with us and thus getting stuck in the agreement trap). In the example above, the couple decided to use a 1–10 scale. If she rated an event or date as a "5 or higher" in importance, he would be on time; if it was less important, she would not worry about him being on time. Of course, in accepting their differences, their ability to be more compassionate about the impact it had on each of them was helpful. He was able to validate her frustration and remind her that she was important to him even if he was late. She was able to appreciate that he valued people and conversations more than being on time and recognize how important she felt when he didn't worry about time when they were talking. Things may not always work out as smoothly as in this example and to be sure, differences can be tricky to accept and navigate. But, if the alternative is getting stuck in the agreement trap and trying to change someone in ways that can feel hurtful, elicit defensiveness, counter-defensiveness, and decrease communication overall, the effort may be worth it.

THE TYRANNY OF "SHOULDS"

How do we know what we want? There are a myriad of complications that make it difficult to identify and communicate what we want and need. We may have grown up in a family where certain needs were mocked, shamed, left unspoken, invisible, or simply unmet. In some circumstances, it may feel too distressing or frightening to identify a need, or too vulnerable, for a variety of reasons, to express a desire directly. Sometimes we think we shouldn't want something so we don't ask. Sometimes the "shoulds" are unconscious; we are unaware that we should ask for something we desire or we're seeking out things we don't want because we think we should want them. Other times, we may be aware of the "shoulds," but because they are too ensnared in guilt or shame we ignore them. For example, if someone believes they are weak for wanting help, or selfish for wanting time alone they are unlikely to ask for those needs to be met because of guilt or shame surrounding the need itself. This not only prevents us from asking for what we want (or saying no to things we don't want), it prompts us to ask in an indirect way. If someone feels guilty, weak, or ashamed about asking for support, they may not ask and suffer alone instead. Or, they may ask indirectly. For example, I worked with a man about the guilt he felt from asking his partner for physical affection. He grew up with the message that asking for (and receiving) physical affection was bad and that he was selfish for wanting it. He overheard the adults in his world make disparaging remarks when people hugged at family gatherings and mocked him when he tried to hold his dad's hand or climb into his lap. It was excruciating for him to ask his partner directly for any physical touch, even though it was extremely soothing and connecting for him. He made implications and discursive attempts at prompting physical touch by talking about how his shoulder hurt or how it was sweet that the couple he saw on his walk to the bus stop was holding hands. His partner, oblivious to the veiled requests, would suggest a hot shower or yoga and agree that it was sweet—not at all what my client wanted. At times, my client told me he would become frustrated and tell his boyfriend that he didn't care about him, that he was cold and unloving. The boyfriend, confused and feeling attacked, countered by saying that he was selfish and demanding, which only served to prove that his childhood messages were "true." When my client was finally able to openly ask for a shoulder rub, or for his boyfriend to hold his hand, he was much more likely to get what he wanted.

It is not always easy to identify and make requests around our needs. How do we get to the root of what we want? How do we discover what hooks our imagination, sparks our soul, makes us tick? How do we know when to listen to that "should" voice and when to ignore it? We don't get there by only acting on what we think we should do. There will always be things we should do and things we think we should do, and things we want but believe we should not want. When we focus primarily on shoulds, life can seem pretty bleak. Life is more dynamic, resilient, and robust when we find balance between wants and shoulds. The REFLECTIVE LOOP is an important tool in exploring and seeking balance (or recognizing imbalance), as it encourages reflection about the various aspects of desires, requests, and boundaries; these include the impact, possible consequences, emotions, thoughts, values, and cultural considerations as well as how all these factors impact and inform one another.

The tyranny of shoulds can also prevent people from developing the skills necessary to accept a need being met, resulting in a push/pull reaction or even in sabotage. In the above example, not only had my client learned to make sideways requests, the guilt and shame he felt about asking for physical touch created a tumultuous and oscillating relationship to his desires. When he received physical touch, a hug or back rub, or other physical affection, he felt guilty and undeserving. He wanted affection but when he got it, it made him feel bad, which made him not want it and sometimes even reject it. His back and forth, or ask/reject as we called it, confused and frustrated his boyfriend, which only seemed to confirm my client's mistaken beliefs that he was selfish.

Shoulds also prevent people from learning how to tolerate their needs *not* being met. Continuing with the above example, when my client did not get physical affection after hinting for it, he felt guilty for asking (even indirectly), rejected, hurt, and angry. Sometimes he lashed out by saying mean things to his boyfriend because he was unable to tolerate his needs not being met. Being able to handle a need not being met is an important skill. If desires or wants are buried under a mountain of shoulds and subsequent judgments, guilt, shame, or other distressing emotions, it becomes difficult to tolerate them not only when they are not being met but also when they *are* being met as well—a double-edged suffering.

There are very real shoulds in life that are important to pay attention to at certain times (*I really should get home to walk the dog*) and ignore at other times (*I shouldn't call my friend to talk, she's probably busy*). Boundary setting, as a negotiation of who and how we are in the world, invites us to reflect on (and communicate) our desires.

LETTING PEOPLE KNOW HOW TO SUPPORT YOU

Another important aspect of the REFLECTIVE LOOP is letting people know how to support you. This means knowing yourself, knowing what you need, and being able to communicate it. After all, you can't tell someone else how to support you if you don't know. Do you want advice? Suggestions? Critiques? Empathic listening? Physical touch? To be left alone? Not to be left alone? What we want and need can change from moment to moment, and sometimes we discover what support is helpful through trial and error. You may start out thinking you want advice only to find out it feels overwhelming. You may ask for constructive criticism and when you get it, you become defensive and realize you were still too emotionally raw or vulnerable for criticism and what you really needed was to be comforted. You can negotiate what you want (setting boundaries) while in the middle of getting support about negotiating boundaries. Circles in circles! It can be helpful to practice asking for and accepting different kinds of support and to explore the various thoughts, feelings, sensations, and action urges that arise as a result.

GIVING SUPPORT

When offering support, it is useful to know what it is the person wants. In the absence of knowing, we may try all kinds of things. We may jump in with great suggestions or ideas on what someone can do to fix their dilemma when all they wanted was some room to cry. We try to soothe someone and they end up feeling like we are shutting them down. We may be ready with tissues and open arms when they want to roll up their sleeves and get busy solving the problem. Some guesses may be on the mark—others, not so much. Sometimes people spend a lot of time guessing what the right thing to do is. One way to save a lot of time and energy is to simply ask. If the person already knows and can communicate it clearly, and you are able to offer the support they want, great. However, there are all sorts of barriers that can get in the way of being able to offer support, including not knowing what the person wants, not having the skills or capacity to ask, not being able to fulfill the need, having fear, and finally, defensiveness.

Mastering the art of offering support requires people to be flexible and able to learn from the times when a need is not clear or the support offered is not helpful. In these moments, it is useful to explore thoughts, feelings, beliefs, sensations, actions, and behaviors with compassionate curiosity, which can offer insight about how to navigate future situations. For example, a client discussed her frustration with her boyfriend. When she came home from work, he would ask about her day and as she shared her frustrations about her supervisor and coworkers, he would inevitably interrupt with helpful suggestions and encouraged her to look for a new job. He routinely reminded her that he would be more than happy to support her while she looked for new work. He thought he was being kind, supportive, and encouraging. She felt shut down and invalidated. When she tried to explain this to him, he became frustrated because to him it seemed like no matter what he did, she never felt better. He was offering her support, to be sure, but it was not the kind of support she wanted and it was making her feel bad, which made him feel discouraged. She and I took some time to explore what it was that she wanted in those moments. Through our discussions, she was able to identify her needs: she wanted to vent without him saying much of anything, and she wanted her frustration and irritation to be validated as justified and reasonable without any problem-solving. When she explained this to her boyfriend, he was not only able to understand that his method of supporting her (problem-solving) was not helpful, he was also able to support her in ways that felt validating and loving for her, which in turn made him feel like an effectual partner.

HOW THE REFLECTIVE LOOP HELPS SUPPORT STRATEGIES FOR BOUNDARY SETTING

At times it can be challenging to explore all the thoughts, feelings, sensations, judgments, desires, values, and secondary and tertiary emotions (i.e., feeling angry about feeling jealous or feeling insecure about feeling lonely) that arise when seeking or offering support, especially when it is not going well. But it is important work. One way to explore this is to be mindful of what comes up in situations. Do you get agitated when someone asks for advice? Are you comfortable with physical soothing but get tongue-tied when someone wants to hash things out? Another strategy is trial and error. Give yourself permission to try out different ways of asking for and offering support. This includes giving yourself permission to "fail," because in order to achieve the goal of improving your ability to ask for what you need and support other people in asking them for what they need, you'll need to be able to offer a variety of different kinds of support. Situations are not static. Different situations with different people will be, well, different. This process is about deepening interpersonal awareness about the complicated nature of identifying and communicating desires; it's about asking for and giving support, not about coming up with a blueprint. Part of increasing awareness is accepting that things may not always go the way we want even when we are being skillful.

TEN

LEARNING SELF-CARE AND SELF-ACCEPTANCE

THIS CHAPTER CONSIDERS RADICAL ACCEPTANCE AS AN IMPORTANT CORE boundary-setting, self-care, and communication tool. In addition, this section will explore a few core concepts for improving self-care and boundary-setting skills, including how cultural norms, power, and privilege impact and inform communication.

SKILLFULNESS IS NOT A FORMULA

Becoming skillful involves trying new things; some will be useful, some will not, and others will depend on context. Failing is part and parcel of gaining mastery or proficiency in a new skill, be it boxing, speaking a second language, tap dancing, writing a poem, or asking for support. Learning to identify what you need requires the ability to tolerate being a beginner (unless this is a skill you are already adept at). If one has a low threshold for making mistakes, learning can be more challenging and distressing, which can motivate one to either seek out formulas for success or avoid new experiences altogether. For example, a child whose environment produces overwhelming stress during times of learning new skills or information will either shut down and avoid these types of situations whenever possible or focus on how to not make mistakes to the exclusion of learning how to learn—how to explore, not know, be curious, and question things from different perspectives. The overwhelming distress in learning moments can be a product of both negative and positive reinforcement. If a child is yelled at when a mistake is made, then they learn to associate errors with stress or anxiety or depression. If, on the other hand, they are overly praised or encouraged after making a mistake, rather than learn how to tolerate the discomfort, distress, or stress associated with being incorrect and developing corrective strategies, the same associations may occur. Either way, the child is more likely to seek out formulas or specific strategies for how to succeed, rather than have a resilient capacity to tolerate the discomfort of not knowing, being a beginner at something, exploring various options, or being inquisitive and explorative about a new skill. While this is a boon for the self-help industry, the inability to explore new ideas or theories, in this case regarding communication and self-care specifically, without striving to have "an answer" or precise methodology delimits one's curiosity and creativity and erodes self-trust. The core concepts discussed below are offered to support examinations of interpersonal communication styles, issues, and barriers while promoting critical reflection, active listening, and evaluative self-trust.

Finding information (or formulas) on improving communication, identifying desires, and negotiating wants and needs is easy. There are books, tapes, videos, and TV shows on improving communication everywhere one turns—it's a self-help supermarket out there with hundreds of different styles and theories to choose from. With the plethora of products offering to help improve communication it can be overwhelming and difficult to know where to begin and what will be useful. While there is not a one-size-fits-all approach to improving communication, there are two core concepts that are important no matter what style or approach people choose. The first is that power cannot be communicated away, and the second is to be aware when using cultural norms to set or explain boundaries.

POWER CANNOT BE COMMUNICATED AWAY

Just about any communication skill or tool can be used to coerce, manipulate, or maintain power and control. Just because someone uses "I" statements or "feeling sentences" or even nonviolent communication skills does not mean they are not misusing power. Power is a very versatile little creature and can sneak in just about anywhere. Using the REFLECTIVE LOOP and being aware of how power is playing out in your relationships is an important and ongoing process. Being mindful of power and power dynamics does not inherently make them go away, but it can inform you about how you choose to communicate, negotiate, and interact in the relationship. There are many ways power enters into relationships. Sometimes differences between partners involves a power dynamic, such as when one partner is a fluent native speaker in the country they live in and the other is not, or one partner is undocumented and the other is not, or one partner owns a car in an environment where it is necessary for transportation while the other one does not. Differences in power are not inherently bad or wrong, but the way they are navigated is important. There are endless ways in which relationships hold differences that translate into social power. One partner may be more comfortable negotiating with institutions and take responsibility for this in the relationship. While this could create a power imbalance in terms of who has more direct access to, or information about, the institutions they are in contact with (e.g., banks, credit unions, utility companies, internet providers, student loan companies, etc.), how the couple communicates and addresses this matters more than the difference itself. If the person who is in direct contact with the institutions uses this to manipulate, isolate, or control their partner then power is being abused. If, however, they communicate and address things in ways that feel equitable to both of them, then it works for that relationship. Power can be misused and abused in countless ways and it is important to not get hooked into believing that any one formula or approach to communication or boundary setting will mitigate it. Power must be grappled with as directly as possible, and this requires practice in identifying power and becoming increasingly more skillful in negotiating and navigating it in relationships. If you are just beginning your journey into understanding privilege and power, consider reading the following articles: "Beyond Inclusion, Beyond Empowerment" by Leticia Nieto; "Anti-Racist Toolkit" by Ignite!; "What is a 'System of Privilege?'" by Allan G. Johnson. The National SEED Project is another wonderful resource.

CULTURAL NORMS

Communication is not only complicated by individual experience, skill, and preference; it is also complicated by cultural norms. Passed on from one generation to the next, cultural norms are the shared, sanctioned, and integrated systems of beliefs, values, and practices that characterize a cultural group. Norms differ from group to group. Navigating differences in cultural norms is an important part of communication and boundary setting. Problems occur when a cultural norm is mistaken for what is "normal" or "right" and the problems are compounded when there is social and institutional power to impose the norm. Modern Western medicine is one example. Many people prefer to use herbs, acupuncture, energy work, and other forms of alternative medicine to treat medical and mental health issues. Most insurance companies elect to not cover "alternative" treatments because they are not considered medically or scientifically established or proven in the way that say an anti-depressant or chemotherapy is. Even the allocation of these practices as being "alternative" is an imposition of a cultural norm, positioning Western medicine at the center from which all other modalities are viewed and evaluated. That certain practices are codified and covered by insurance is based on cultural norms surrounding how to define and treat medical and mental health issues, and on what evidence is considered necessary to prove efficacy. If someone is unable to access alternative or holistic treatments because their insurance won't cover it and they can't afford care without insurance, that is an example of a cultural norm being imposed because it is seen as right or normal. In this way, some cultural norms are upheld over others and at times reflect the systemic issues of classism, racism, homophobia, transphobia, sexism, ableism, and other forms of marginalization and oppression.

At an individual level, if you believe that not raising your voice when you argue with your partner is a "good" communication style and you frame your boundary as the normal way of doing things, you are imposing your cultural norm and values onto your partner rather than negotiating your boundary. Not everyone feels uncomfortable around loud voices and yelling. In fact, for some people or within some families, communities, and cultures, raising your voice implies passion—not anger. The goal is to be mindful and intentional when using cultural norms or social rules and expectations to explain boundaries. A great resource for becoming aware of power, cultural norms, and how they can be invisible is Peggy McIntosh's article "White Privilege and Male Privilege: A Personal Account of Coming to See Correspondences Through Work in Women's Studies" (1988). You can also check out The People's Institute for Survival and Beyond.

HOLDING VS. DEFENDING YOUR BOUNDARY

You don't always have to defend your boundary; sometimes you only need to hold it. People can get so caught up in defending a boundary that they don't pay attention to what is happening in the moment. A simple but challenging strategy is to see what the other person's response is rather than anticipate it. Set a boundary and pause, wait and see what happens, and then respond to that, rather than to what you think might happen. When we leap ahead, it is easy to make assumptions and mistakes. There are humorous examples from everyday life when one person asks for something and the other person says yes right away but the person arguing for their want is so busy explaining *why* the other person should say yes that they don't even hear the yes and keep explaining. Pausing helps unhook us when we get caught up in emotions, thoughts, and anticipated reactions. Pausing can be challenging, especially if the situation is emotionally charged.

One practice is to link pauses with breath, with taking a long, deep breath to help you slow down or remind you to be present. This involves taking a breath and bringing attention completely to your breath before focusing on what is happening in the moment and deciding on any action or response. It is helpful in the beginning to practice this stop-breathe-pause tactic in neutral or low stakes situations. The more practice people have in remembering to stop, breathe, pause, and then respond in less intense moments, the easier it will be to do it in more intense situations. The pause is not simply a moment to think about what you are going to say or do; it is about intentionally slowing down and bringing oneself into the present moment in order to respond more effectively. There is a lot happening in interpersonal interactions, including what is being said, nonverbal communication, thoughts, feelings, and sensations; being able to direct attention enables people to be more in the present moment and respond to what is actually happening rather than react to what is anticipated, feared, or hoped for.

RADICAL ACCEPTANCE

Radical acceptance is another tool that helps people stay present and respond rather than react. Radical acceptance is not a passive *that's just the way it is, there's nothing I can do* kind of acceptance. It is a very active and participatory stance, rooted in reality. It's accepting things as they are, rather than getting stuck in how you wish things were. Wishing things were different is an easy place to go. There are things in life that suck. There are things that are unfair, painful, and devastating. Accepting them does not mean we don't work to change or avoid what we are able to. It means accepting things as they are now, which is not always a pleasant endeavor. But not doing so adds suffering to the very real pain that is already present, which inevitably makes things worse. There are numerous research studies on how mindfulness practices reduce stress, anxiety, and physical and emotional pain. The Mayo Clinic has done extensive research studies on the effects of mindfulness on pain and stress reduction. Mindfulness is the act of being aware of thoughts, feelings, sensations, and action urges, without judging, meaning-making, or interpreting. Radical acceptance extends mindfulness to the world around us and is the acceptance of what *is,* in this very moment, without getting mired in how something is unfair or unjust—even if it is. Radical acceptance is rooted in the here and now, in the present moment, not the future or the past. When one accepts (radically) an unfair or unjust situation, the acceptance is not about accepting that it will be this way forever (sometimes it may be, sometimes it may not), but about accepting the reality of how things are now, in this moment. This type of acceptance offers a grounded place from which one can decide how to respond and enact whatever change is possible. Radical acceptance of painful, unjust, unforgivable, prejudiced, oppressive, or undesired events or circumstances allows one to be more responsive and less reactive, which supports rather than demarks possibilities for change.

A client came to me expressing his desire to stop feeling stuck. His father died before they had a chance to reconcile. He felt guilty, ashamed, angry, and trapped. He had hoped for an opportunity to talk with his father and see if it would be possible to forgive him, but now that opportunity was gone forever. Unsure how to live with his resentment, anger, and guilt, my client was suffering a great deal. His relationship had recently ended, and badly at that, and he was at risk of losing his job. He was miserable but saw no way out. As we discussed his feelings and possible options it became clear that he was ensnared in emotional turmoil: he couldn't undo the past and he couldn't forgive himself or his father; he could not tolerate his guilt but he felt like he deserved it so he could not let go of it. He was angry with his father but since he was gone, my client felt stuck with his anger; he was resentful toward his father for dying and guilty about feeling resentful. As we spent time together, we began to explore the idea of radical acceptance. The goal was not forgiveness but to reduce his suffering somewhat so that he could be more engaged in his life. In this case, radical acceptance involved my client accepting the reality that the possibility of him reconciling with his father before his father died was gone. Forever. He could engage in various healing practices, but he would never be able to reconcile with his dad in "real life" as he put it. The grief and loss he experienced in accepting this was overwhelming, as grief often is, and we spent a great deal of time doing grief work together in the process of him grappling with the concept of radical acceptance. As he came to accept the painful concreteness of his father's passing and the certainty that "real life" reconciliation was not possible, he was able to feel other emotions, make room for other memories of him and his father, and this in turn allowed him to be more present in his current life. No factual things changed during our work together. His father was still gone and the reconciliation had still not occurred, but my client was no longer stuck in the suffering of wanting things to be different—he accepted with a great deal of pain that things were the way the were and the only thing he could do was either choose to accept them and decide how to move forward, or to not accept them and be wed to his guilt and shame forever. It was not a great choice and either way my client would feel painful and distressing emotions, but not accepting things as they were only would only add more agony to an already difficult situation.

Radical acceptance asks people to feel emotions that they are often desperate to not feel, and no matter the intellectual understanding that refusing to accept things as they are won't actually change things, people may still cling to the hope that nonacceptance will stop or dull the pain. It does not. Facing a painful reality is difficult so it is understandable that people do not want to or sometimes refuse to. But not facing reality prevents one from being present and fully engaged with life, which, while extraordinarily painful at times, can also be amazingly wonderful and glorious.

Accepting things as they are so that we can work to make the changes we want to and are able of making is challenging. Sometimes it involves painful grief work, as in the above example. Other times, radical acceptance involves a subtler shift in our perspective or paradigm. This shift is not always easy. There is a story in the book *The Song of the Bird* by spiritual teacher Anthony de Mello. It's a story shared by many Zen teachers, and Martha Linehan uses it in her workbook for facilitating Dialectical Behavioral Therapy groups. The story is helpful and bears repeating. The following excerpt is an adapted version:

A man bought a new house and decided that he wanted a beautiful and perfect lawn. He worked on it every week, doing everything the gardening books told him to do. The big problem was the lawn had dandelions that didn't seem to ever go away. The first time he found dandelions, he pulled them out. They grew back. He went to a gardening store and bought weed killer. The dandelions shriveled and died. He thought he was done with this dilemma, but to his dismay the dandelions grew back. He pulled them all out again, working very hard every weekend. The next summer he thought he would finally be free of his dandelions since none grew back during the winter. But alas, the summer came and dandelions popped up all over his lawn! He then decided it must be the type of grass he had. He spent a fortune and had all new grass put down. This worked for some time and the man was very happy. Just as he started to relax, however, the dandelions came back. A friend told him this was due to the dandelions in the lawn next door. The man went on a campaign to get all of his neighbors to kill all their dandelions. By the third year he was exhausted and he still had dandelions. After consulting every expert and book he could find he decided to write the U.S. Department of Agriculture for advice. Surely they could help. After several months he finally received a reply. He was very excited. He tore the letter open and read the following: "Dear Sir: We have considered your problem and have consulted all of our experts. After careful consideration, we think we can give you very good advice. Sir, our advice is that you learn to love those dandelions.

Exploring what we want often means finding love, contentment, and happiness in places we may have never thought possible. It involves paying attention inwardly as well as externally, outside ourselves. If we are so focused on weeds, we miss the joy of being outside in the sun working on our lawn (or even enjoying lovely yellow dandelions). If we only focus on the imperfect or the painful, trying desperately to make it go away, it sabotages our joy. When we are feeling happy, we worry about when it will be over. When the lawn is free from dandelions, we are happy, but as soon as one pops up, we are frustrated. This is expecting our life, like the lawn, to be perfect and basing our happiness on achieving perfection. It is easy to look to an idea of what it is to be happy or perfect (we are bombarded by advertising and branding messages relentlessly) and then cling desperately to it—like a perfect lawn. It is not difficult to become lured into thinking happiness exists outside of ourselves. Happiness then becomes confused with a state of emotion obtained by external things like the perfect lawn, a pair of shoes, a specific relationship, or the right job. None of these things are bad. They are also not good. They are, in fact, neutral. Rather, it is our belief that they are connected to happiness and the meaning assigned to them that causes so much suffering. When we get what we want, we fear losing it. When we don't get what we want, we are upset and long for it. This locates joy outside of ourselves and places responsibility for happiness on external things rather than on our perspective or beliefs, which in turn distances us from our internal landscape of feelings and experience. This also makes setting and negotiating boundaries more about trying to achieve and maintain an ideal of happiness or perfection, rather than about grappling with the messy reality of confusing and sometimes conflicting wants and needs. It can also make us equate "good" boundaries with "perfect" boundaries. That is, with boundaries that are set exactly how we want them and are responded to in the precise way we imagined.

Over time, an externally focused ideal of happiness can result in people being out of tune with their own feelings and bodies—what they need and want—and the ability to direct attention, focus, and experience in the service of what they need. In this outwardly focused paradigm, turning inward, listening to one's self, and locating happiness inside one's self becomes a radical act.

Radical Acceptance and Boundary Setting

How do boundaries fit into the struggle to have a perfect lawn, let go of unrealistic expectations, or accept a painful circumstance? Boundaries are a means to ask for or negotiate wants and needs, to accept things, and to change things. When boundaries are set or negotiated from a place of radical acceptance, they are rooted in the reality of what *is* and what is possible. This, in turn, means that they are more likely to be based on what people really want and need rather than what people think they should or shouldn't want (which results in happier, healthier, and more resilient people, environments, and relationships). Trying to negotiate a need that cannot be met or that a person feels they shouldn't have can quickly become a tangle of emotions, desires, beliefs, values, thoughts, and judgments. Radical acceptance helps untangle the knots because it involves naming or noticing and accepting each element before deciding what to do. When someone can accept a need as well as the various (and sometimes contradictory) feelings, thoughts, values, beliefs, and action urges that accompany the need, they will be better equipped to explore how they want to respond. For example, if someone wants to ask for support but believes they should be able to handle things themselves, they often position these two as oppositional: *either I ask for support or do things myself.* Meaning is also typically assigned to each approach: *asking for help is bad. Getting support means I am weak. Doing things on my own is how I let people know I won't be a burden.* Radical acceptance of both of these beliefs and desires as well as thoughts, judgments, meanings, values, beliefs, and action urges, offers a way out of the contradictory loop (*either I ask for support and am weak or I go at it alone and am not a burden*). Radical acceptance opens up possibilities that collapse when people are unable or unwilling to accept the circumstances at hand. In the above example, radical acceptance helps the person decide what they want to do in response to a situation where they want help but also want to go at it alone. Radical acceptance also helps them accept the reality that either decision will result in feeling some distressing emotions. Using radical acceptance, they can explore additional feelings or aspects of the particular circumstances and then decide in that moment what the best next step for them is. Radical acceptance creates a path through seemingly contradictory stances, disentangles them from one another, and asks that responses be based on what is possible given the reality of that particular moment. This allows people to navigate difficult emotional, psychological, and environmental circumstances more skillfully. In this way, radical acceptance supports more effective boundary setting. If you are dealing with things as they really are rather than how you wish things would be, or think they should be, responses are more connected to what is actually happening in the moment. Through acceptance, like learning to love dandelions, people will find new ways of setting boundaries and even discover new boundaries themselves.

Radical acceptance helps us negotiate boundaries that are rooted in both the reality of the world we live in and in the truth of which needs and wants are important and possible. This supports stronger, more vibrant, and resilient relationships and communities. The reality is that inequities, injustices, prejudices, and malfeasance hurt people at an individual and social level on a daily basis. We live in a world where rich people live longer, white people still have better access to health care, men continue to dominate financially and politically, gay, lesbian, trans and genderqueer people are bullied, people of color are targets of racism and discrimination, domestic violence persists, sexual abuse is still a pervasive reality, and prisons are a business market niche. Our little planet is warming with a fever that those in power (in the United States) are ignoring with disastrous implications.

We have a lot of work to do. That doesn't let us off the hook for finding and creating our own happiness. An important aspect of this kind of boundary work is that it helps people be happier, calmer, more confident, compassionate, and grounded in how to advocate for their wants and needs.

ELEVEN

COMMUNITY CARE AND SOCIAL CHANGE

THAT'S (NOT) JUST THE WAY IT IS

"THAT'S JUST THE WAY IT IS." IN MY MIND, THIS PHRASE IS A WAY TO justify giving up. It's a verbal version of palms extended in the air in a surrendering gesture. Boundaries are about self-care. Self-care is connected to relationship care, community care, neighborhood care, neighbor care, global-neighbor care, and planetary care. It is critical that we all participate in taking care of the earth and the people that inhabit our precious planet. If I believe that women should not be coerced, manipulated, or beaten into having sex then it is important for me to not only learn how to stand up for my own boundaries as a woman, but also to promote, encourage, and participate in creating environments, conditions, and relationships that do not perpetuate violence against women. When someone responds to incidents of harm or abuse with an equivalent of "That's just the way it is," in essence they are saying that there is nothing to be done to change things and are, perhaps more importantly, allowing themselves a way to not feel guilty about their inaction. We not only need to do something, it is imperative that we *feel* like we need to do something. Our ability to adapt to unhealthy environments and oppressive systems can numb us and limit imaginative and creative alternatives to current conditions. To not be numb is to feel an urgent need to do something to change things.

If I want to numb out with television, booze, shopping, prescription or nonprescription drugs, food, or any of the other things we can use to divert our attention away from deep and meaningful self-care and the work required to change the conditions in which violence and abuse occur, that's a choice I get to make. Too often we don't view a lack of participation as an active choice. We throw up our hands and say, "That's just the way it is." This excuses us quite neatly from having to *do* anything. In order to change things, we have to choose to participate, which is not always easy, as participation can be extraordinarily painful. Participation means grappling with how deeply entrenched victim blaming is in many of our social (and individual) responses to harm. It also involves looking at all the various and complicated factors that contribute to violence, abuse, and harm. Participation means looking at the privilege of being able to choose to not participate. Victim blaming, or "pathologizing" and criminalizing, those who engage in certain kinds of harm does not call for a deep investigation of the conditions that contribute to violence and how we in the United States respond to it.

FROM SELF-CARE TO COMMUNITY CARE

Mainstream concepts around meeting needs or setting boundaries tend to be rooted in the individual self (*I want to feel safe, I want to be loved, I want to feel secure, I need you to listen more, I need a hug, I need to be respected*). In reality, the whole point of getting what we want, of negotiating our boundaries, is about being more connected to other people and the world. Boundaries occur in connection to other people. Even when we are setting boundaries located only within ourselves (*I will limit myself to one sweet treat a week, I will bike to work most days, I will try to smile more*), we are doing so in social and relational contexts. We depend on one another in very deep and complex ways, yet most boundary discussions are focused on how to cut off or distance our-selves from unwanted behaviors or people. In chapter two, we looked at how boundary work is just as much about negotiating and asking for what we want and need as what we don't want and don't need. To this end, if we are working toward not just our own individual safety but toward changing the conditions in which people are not safe or are being harmed, then boundaries are about imagining radical possibili-ties as much as responding to events in the present.

REFLECTING ON SAFETY AS AN INDIVIDUAL RIGHT

In some contexts, boundaries are positioned as a personal, individual right. In self-defense classes, I have heard teachers describe safety as a personal right that women need to claim. To some degree, this is true. Women do deserve to live in a world where they are safe—we all do—and there is much work to be done toward creating that reality. But carving out safety as an individual right tends to place responsibility for safety solely on the individual rather than on the various factors and conditions that cause or perpetuate that which people are trying to protect themselves from. When we centralize safety around the concept of individual rights and focus on the behavior of individual boundary transgressors or perpetrators, while simultaneously ignor-ing the complexities of factors in which violence and abuse occur, we often end up reacting to individual acts of violence while ignoring violence as a larger social issue.

For example, arresting male students accused of sexual assault on a college campus without there being a larger community response to sexism, gender and gender-based violence, male privilege, and social systems that contribute to misogyny on campus. Another example comes from my early work with Home Alive. A bartender responded to a customer's racist remark by eighty-sixing him (i.e., telling him to leave) and letting him know he was not welcome back. While laudable, we dialogued with the bartender and staff, asking them to consider a more holistic response that could address the larger social conditions; to consider the various ways in which staff and customers were made to feel unsafe and impacted by sexism, transphobia, homophobia, or racism, and how they could be supported. The staff agreed and a series of meetings were held at the bar with staff and community members. Through these conversations people developed a number of creative responses. These included offering a series of workshops, hosting events at the bar, and posting signs in all the bars in that neighborhood stating clearly that bigotry of any kind was not acceptable and that staff would intervene and respond to all incidents of bigotry. During this series of talks with bartenders and club staff, they asked about how to identify and intervene in situations that may involve domestic violence. This led to another round of community trainings with creative solutions, including posting artwork and resource information in bathrooms and having staff trainings about community resources. The staff began having conversations with regulars about violence and abuse in relationships, and groups of men began to talk with other men about how to interrupt "bad" behavior, as they put it, among their peers.

In another instance, a woman was raped in the bathroom of a club. Community members responded by offering trainings to club staff around responding to sexual assault and supporting survivors. The club organized benefit shows with proceeds going to sexual assault advocacy programs. In addition, the club posted literature with local sexual assault resources, ways to organize community responses, and accountability processes. A local artist curated an art show in the bathroom where the assault occurred. Patrons of the bar organized cab fare funds and coordinated rides home for women.

These ongoing discussions helped create larger community backdrops that enabled people to respond to individual acts of violence in ways that interrupted victim blaming, worked to hold people accountable, addressed multiple intersecting issues and social systems, and changed the environment in which violence occurred while creating a number of creative responses. None of this was perfect by any means and there were ongoing discussions about problems, concerns, and issues that arose throughout. One factor we continually faced was that when social conditions are considered, they are often viewed as easily remedied through punitive or policy-oriented measures that do not seek to radically transform. Punishing people who engage in domestic violence through arrest and criminal proceedings is one example. This approach to safety is individual-focused (both on the individual survivor and on the abuser) and responsive to the violence itself but does not focus a great deal on transforming the social and cultural systems that contribute to interpersonal violence. The organizations NW Network of Bi, Trans, Lesbian, and Gay Survivors of Abuse and generationFIVE both have amazing, informative resources about how to respond to violence and abuse in transformative ways.

WE SHOULDN'T ALWAYS WANT TO FEEL COMFORTABLE

It is important that people are able to prioritize their own safety and well-being. It is also critical that situating safety as an individual right does not curtail our capacity to tolerate things that are undesirable or uncomfortable. This is different from enduring abusive, unsafe, dangerous situations or controlling behaviors. The complex reality is that we live in social environments full of adverse (as well as wonderful) interpersonal and social situations. If the primary tools for dealing with unwanted behaviors or undesirable people is to cut them off, push them away, punish them, or sever the relationship entirely in order to assert our right to be safe, then the opportunity to develop the skills necessary to navigate those moments of hurt or difference, the moments of holding firm with our boundary while holding onto relationships, becomes limited. It positions safety as oppositional, which is not inherently bad but important to be mindful of nonetheless.

A student in a six-week self-defense class asked if they could write the phrase, "My safety is more important than someone's feelings" on the board before each class. The rest of the students liked the idea and so they wrote it on the dry-erase board each night. We used this statement as a way for the class to consider various aspects and the complex contexts of self-defense and boundary setting. There will be times, for sure, when we will not care about hurting a person's feelings when setting a boundary. But there will also be times when we will care very much. How people have been taught by their family and social conditioning to consider (or not) people's feelings will inform their relationship to the statement. For some people, learning to *not* consider someone else's feelings will be a radically transformative and empowering act. For others, learning to consider how their choices impact others may be enlightening and transformative. The class used the ongoing discussion of the student's statement to explore how situating individual safety is informed by social conditions, and how prioritizing individual safety can be empowering as well as a mechanism to assert power over someone else in ways that mirror systems of privilege.

In boundary-setting classes, participants often talk about how technology makes some people feel safer. A woman shared how having an iPod has helped her feel more confident about setting boundaries because she doesn't have to return unwanted gazes when she is wearing earbuds. She explained that the earbuds make her feel comfortable about not talking to people because she can simply gesture that she can't hear them if someone were to try to engage her in conversation. This is great way for her to take care of herself. But relying primarily on avoiding contact with unwanted people and conversations can isolate us and deprive us of the social and boundary skills we need when we do interact with people who push our buttons or make us uncomfortable. We shouldn't want to always feel safe and comfortable. If that's the goal, we are not pushing ourselves outside of our comfort zone, which is necessary to build a life worth living. Whether it is challenging yourself to do something scary, sustaining a friendship, starting a new relationship, mourning the loss of someone important, facing immortality, accepting an unfortunate event, advocating for social change, learning about systemic inequities and the various privileges we may hold—life is full of situations that challenge people to enter into uncomfortable and sometimes even unsafe territory. Boundaries are a tool to help navigate these circumstances more skillfully (and to avoid them when prudent to do so).

Boundaries help people manage the complicated realm of relationships and social interactions and support people learning ways to keep themselves safe without living in fear. Boundaries, in this way, allow people to move into uncomfortable, messy situations (where mistakes are inevitable) with enough interpersonal resiliency to learn and grow from them. Boundaries are about holding ourselves accountable while negotiating who and how we are in the world, which means being in the world more, not less. Of course, there are days where you just want to slap on your headphones and ignore everyone while you take the bus home after a long day. That's a fine choice. The goal of this type of boundary setting is to have options so that people can be both grounded and spontaneous and be able to identify and communicate needs and wants rather than relying on formulaic action plans. This kind of boundary work encourages people to trust themselves without thinking that some day they will no longer make mistakes. Finally, setting boundaries from this framework allows people to prioritize individual wants and needs while holding the complex reality that they exist in a world where everyone is connected, thus underscoring the importance of linking self-care to social and community care.

CONNECTIONS AND INTERSECTIONS OF INDIVIDUAL AND COMMUNITY SAFETY

Linking self-care to community care means connecting individual safety to the safety of others. This does not necessarily translate directly into surviving the same kind of harm or grappling with the same abuses or violence—just because someone or a community as a whole is being targeted or surviving violence or abuse does not mean that *I* am unsafe. However, it would hopefully inform how I choose to respond. If a community in a different time zone has been traumatized because their water supply is poisoned, or a neighborhood across the state is struggling to protect themselves from police brutality, or I read about a woman being raped in my city, and I believe my safety is deeply connected to the safety of others, then their safety and well-being becomes part of my agenda. If their safety is part of my agenda, then I pay attention when they are not safe. This does not mean reacting to each and every incident of harm or abuse with equal measure. There will be many instances where I will not have the skills, knowledge, experience, capacity, resources, or even the invitation to respond. But it is important to consider and to connect my work in setting and negotiating my own boundaries to the well-being of other people when possible. I may choose to prioritize water safety and organize against the privatization of water, for example, or support my local Mothers Against Police Brutality organization, or offer workshops on issues connected to identifying and interrupting sexism at my workplace.

When other people are not safe or are targets of interpersonal or systemic violence, aggression, or abuse, I am affected. I may not be a direct target of the specific act of violence that is occurring, but I am affected nonetheless. Being affected is not the same as being the target or having to survive or grapple with the violence and abuse. There are a few ways in which I am affected. If I allow for others to be treated poorly, I allow for the possibility that I will be treated in the same manner. That I am not treated in the same manner may speak to my privilege, but it is not a testament to my immunity. We need only look to history for confirmation. When a woman is raped, it is not only she who is impacted. Other women, friends, family, acquaintances, and strangers alike are reminded of the ever-present potential threat of sexual violence that all kinds of women learn to live with. Women can be traumatized and triggered by hearing about violence against another woman. When a trans person is assaulted on the street, fear radiates throughout the community. Every genderqueer and genderqueer-looking person is reminded of how they may be targeted. This kind of harm affects those not directly impacted by reinforcing particular norms and standards and stoking fear and anxiety that can lead to victim blaming. Victim blaming makes all of us less safe because it constructs an individualistic social and cultural paradigm around both violence survival and self-care that isolates and separates us from one another and positions us as potential adversaries. Boundary work that is grounded in the commitment to linking self-care to social and community care redirects responsibility from those surviving the harm to the people choosing to engage in harm and to the conditions (social, political, historical, economic, structural) that contribute to the harm occurring.

ROOTING BOUNDARIES IN OUR NEEDS AND THE LARGER WORLD WE LIVE IN

If boundaries are a negotiation of who and how we are in the world, and if we believe our self-care and well-being are connected to the self-care and well-being of others, then how we set our boundaries needs to be rooted in a larger sense of the world we live in—not just in our individual lives. How and when I choose to set a boundary is connected to my personal safety and may impact others. For example, there are many different responses in the classes I teach about when or if to call the police. Different people and different communities have very different relationships to police. For some communities, the presence of police is reassuring. In others, police presence can be threatening and intimidating. Some people in class have chosen to call the police when they witnessed domestic violence, while others have reasoned that bringing police to the scene could make things less safe, especially for the survivor. Class participants have talked about how calling the police when witnessing domestic violence is a way to set a boundary for themselves—a visible and tangible signal that relationship violence will not be tolerated by them.

Boundaries are not isolated from the environment in which they occur. If I have the power and privilege to impose what I think is best (calling the police) and I impose it (calling the police) without being aware of the possible ramifications that my actions may have, then my boundaries could result in harm to someone or reproduce or reinforce harmful and oppressive systems. Transformative Justice provides a working model for responding to conflicts, engaging community members, using a systems approach, and working independently from traditional institutional responses.

As we expand the concept of boundaries to be deeply connected to the well-being of others, it is important that we see others and ourselves in the complex social context we all live in. We get to use whatever boundaries we can to keep ourselves safe. The larger goal, however, is to not set boundaries that reproduce harm (unless that is the intention) or keep us safe through victim blaming or reproducing systems of inequity. We need to expand our repertoire and strive to keep ourselves safe and set boundaries in ways that do *not* uphold systems that value some people's safety more than others. There will always be times when we fall back on victim-blaming myths and stereotypes we have learned or rely on and access social systems and resources that adversely impact some people and communities. It's inevitable that we will be products of our environments and conditioning, and the reality is that the institutions and social systems currently in place are complicated and entrenched in inequities. What is not inevitable is how things can be. We have the power to change how we participate in our relationships and in our social environments through boundaries. We have the power to recognize that our health and happiness are linked inextricably to that of others. We have the power to choose to set and negotiate boundaries in ways that uphold our needs, value other people, and address the conditions and context that inform our boundaries. We choose how we are going to participate in our environments and our relationships. Let's choose to participate in ways that strive to let everyone participate. Our work and our boundaries will not be perfect, but when we approach boundary setting within a framework that recognizes the larger social conditions, and in a way that reflects a commitment to valuing all of us, radical transformation is possible.

TWELVE

WRAPPING IT ALL UP

THERE ARE MANY DIFFERENT TOOLS FOR BOUNDARY SETTING AND self-care. This book focuses on some core skills that I believe are helpful in most situations for most people. They are not a quick fix or a sure shot for setting effective boundaries. They are part of a repertoire of tools that I hope you will continue to expand on. I also hope that increasing the number of tools you have also includes looking at all the things you have been doing. It is easy, so easy, to look back on times we didn't set the boundary we wanted or didn't handle a situation in the way we would have liked and beat ourselves up for it. We judge and shame ourselves ruthlessly. This does not facilitate a learning environment. In addition, it makes all the amazing things we have done invisible. We need to celebrate the amazing things we do. We need to learn how to celebrate our "mistakes," and extract the moments of learning out of them, and also, more importantly, discover how to be loving and compassionate with ourselves. The REFLECTIVE LOOP is not a tool to use to beat ourselves up with for not doing something well or "right." It's a compassionate tool that helps us challenge ourselves, hold ourselves accountable with patience and forgiveness. This shift in perspective is important. This perspective creates the framework from which we choose self-defense, boundary-setting, and self-care tools that do not perpetuate victim blaming, that let our true selves shine, and allows us to be the complex, creative, and resourceful individuals that we are.

We get to choose the tools that will work for us. Everyone will choose different tools at different times and use them differently. Whether it's NAME THE BEHAVIOR, GIVE A DIRECTIVE, the BROKEN RECORD, or END AN INTERACTION, our situations will all look different when implementing them. Everyone has a different relationship to their intuition and different barriers to trusting it. We will all use the REFLECTIVE LOOP in various ways and be at different places with it. Some of us are just starting to build a support system, others are deepening the support they already have, while others may have been using a tool like this for a long time and are simply revisiting it as part of boundary work. There is not a better or "right" place to be in our boundary work. It's a process, and wherever you are, you won't stay there forever—that's the nature of process! All the tools we've discussed—NAME THE BEHAVIOR; GIVE A DIRECTIVE; BROKEN RECORD; REFLECTIVE LOOP; intuition; building, using, and nurturing a support system; practicing accountability; and forgiveness—keep evolving as we do. We are not static beings. We, like our boundaries, will constantly be growing, learning, changing, and adapting.

This ever-evolving process is rooted in discovering our own happiness. Not just an individual happiness that we are taught to seek out (mostly through new and improved gadgets and accessories), but rather a deep contentment that can hold steady when things get stormy—because they will. A deep sense of connection to how our well-being is tied to the health and well-being of our communities at a local, national, and international level. Rather than making us feel overwhelmed and as a result, isolated and complacent, this realization of connection can inspire and motivate us. It means that while we are all individuals who will set boundaries differently, we are also all part of a larger web of humanity. The distance between others and us is not so great as to be insurmountable or unimaginable. Our gift and our responsibility is to imagine. To realize my safety and well-being are linked to others' is an amazing thing. When someone keeps himself or herself safe without blaming the victim, I, too, am safer.

One of the things I am very proud of achieving in my life is helping create Home Alive. I had the amazing opportunity to grow and mature as a facilitator, activist, artist, writer, and survivor. My exploration and boundary work have been an important part of my own healing, and these have helped me become a deeply passionate and committed supporter of healing work, both personally and professionally. One of the great joys of teaching were the "Aha" moments I got to witness class participants have: those moments where a person's personal paradigm shifts as they integrate the information more deeply in ways that work for them.

It is my hope that you had and will continue to have some "light bulb moments" of insight and awareness that enable you to go deeper into boundary and self-care work as an individual, as a community member, and as a living being on this planet. I am humbled by all the examples I have seen of people making these connections and doing work that reflects the belief and value that we are all connected and that we all have to take care of each other as well as ourselves. Home Alive was founded on such values. We began because we saw the need to take care of each other. We believed from the beginning that violence is a community responsibility. That we have to shift the focus away from fear-based, blame-the-victim responses to a more liberation-oriented mindset that helps us imagine our lives, our relationships, and our world without violence. That doesn't mean we don't stay grounded in the reality that we live in a world that often perpetuates violence. We can use self-defense and boundary-setting skills to interrupt violence in the moment. We can also use them to negotiate the kinds of environments where violence is less likely to happen. These are not separate nor mutually exclusive—in fact, both are necessary.

It is challenging to not get hooked by fear. Fear permeates our landscape to such a large degree that it can seem imperceptible yet ever present. When we turn on the news, read the headlines, or reflect on the things our friends and families or ourselves go through, it is tough to not feel helpless. Helplessness can make us grasp for a quick fix. We must resist this urge. We must keep learning how to resist it and work to be compassionate with ourselves, especially in the moments we feel unable to. Through compassion, we can move past those moments of fear and helplessness and into our courage and tremendous capacity.

Boundary setting is about who and how we are in the world. This means staying present in the current moment, understanding our past, and looking to the future. It means being bold, envisioning how you want to be and what kind of world you want to be in.

EXERCISES

///////////////////////////////

BELOW ARE A FEW DIFFERENT EXERCISES I HAVE USED IN CLASSES AND workshops. They build on the material in the book, and while it is not necessary to read the book in order to use the exercises, I have made notes for when it may be helpful to reference chapter material.

THE RELATIONSHIP SOLAR SYSTEM

This exercise has come from a variety of sources in a variety of formats. I have seen it facilitated in different ways by tremendously talented teachers and facilitators, including all the amazing Home Alive instructors who brought to it their own expertise and experience. There is also a similar exercise in *The Courage to Trust* by Cynthia L. Wall. The "Relationship Solar System" exercise helps you create a visual image or snapshot of the various relationships in your life. Start by listing the various people in your life and then place them on a "solar system," with you in the center. This exercise is a tool to help you reflect on the relationships you have in your life at the present moment. There is no "right" kind of solar system and there is no right way to create and draw one. Have fun and be creative. This is a tool to help you grow and learn, not to doubt your abilities or beat yourself up.

You can do this exercise whenever you want to get a snapshot of the people in your life. Some people find it helpful to do on a regular basis while others do it when they are reflecting on something specific.

Use it in whatever way works best for you. Play with it. There are many different versions of this exercise and it is always being redeveloped and modified as facilitators and participants adapt it to work for their particular focus. This is not about doing something right; it's about having another tool for us to get to know ourselves and our relationships so we can make informed choices about what we need and want.

SETTING UP THE SOLAR SYSTEM

1. First, brainstorm all the different types of relationships you have in your life and write them on a piece of paper. Types of relationships may include personal, family, acquaintances, friends, people in your social networks, mentors, teachers, supervisors, coworkers, people you volunteer with, and the service industry (people you serve or those who serve you, such as baristas, beauticians, consultants, coaches, counselors, or body workers).

2. Next, on a separate piece of paper, using the different types of relationships as your guide, list people who are in your life at the present moment. You can make columns with the different types of relationships as headings, or you can create a list in whatever way works for you. You don't have to include every person who fits in each relationship category. And you don't have to go through every relationship category. You can if that works for you, but if you get stuck in trying to fill in every category or begin to feel overwhelmed by including every person, ease up. The goal of this is to get you thinking about the various types of relationships you have in your life and some of the people who make up the different types of relationships, not to draft a comprehensive list of every person who makes up your solar system.

3. Next, take another blank sheet of paper and draw yourself in the center. If drawing yourself feels stressful, you can use a symbol or a stick figure or simply write your name—aesthetics

are not important (unless that is helpful for you). It is simply a useful, visual snapshot of the relationships in your world. After you have drawn yourself in the center, draw circles around yourself, moving from the center outward, like the rings in a solar system. There are no rules for how many rings you draw, but most people draw 3–5 as a place to start. The rings represent the degrees or differences in our relationships. The closer the ring is to your center, the closer the person is to you. Closeness, of course, is subjective—people can be physically close but emotionally distant. Or there may be people in our lives with whom we are very intimate but who live far away. We will explore more when we place people on our solar system.

4. Now that you have your solar system map, it's time to place people from your list on it. There is not a right way to begin, just start putting people on your solar system in the place that feels right to you in this moment. Remember, this is not a permanent image of how your relationships are; it's a snapshot of how you see things today. As mentioned above, there are times when someone may be close yet distant; in that case, place that person where you think they should go *today*. If in this moment a friend feels very far away even though they live with you, you may put them on or near the second or third ring. Tomorrow it may be different. You may have just had a very intimate talk with a new friend or a fight with your brother. You may be feeling close with your coworkers but don't see them outside of work. People's degree of intimacy, importance, presence, and closeness will vary. People in the same category will be very different from each other. We are not close in the same way with every friend, for example. Even the categories people are in may change over time. For example, strangers become friends, friends become partners, acquaintances become mentors, and supervisors become friends. Again, there isn't a right place to put people; this exercise is about asking yourself where you feel they should be in this moment.

5. Once you have completed your solar system, you will be using different color pens, pencils, or markers to signify the types of relationships represented. You can circle friendships, underline work relationships, put a star next to family, and a dot under acquaintances ... use whatever symbols and colors work for you.

6. After signifying different types of relationships, you will again use different color pens, pencils, or markers to identify relationship dynamics. For example, conflicted, supportive (you provide support, they provide support, or both), full of admiration, joyful, constricting, nurturing, healing, tense, loving, casual, serious, argumentative, challenging, painful, scary, critical, warm, friendly, awkward. You can use red squiggly lines for conflict and yellow thick lines for supportive. Again, use colors and symbols that work for you.

7. Now it's time to reflect on your solar system. Listed below are some questions to get you started, followed by a few writing exercises:

   ♦ What do you notice first when you look at your solar system?

   ♦ What thoughts and emotions come up?

   ♦ Are there places or patterns on your solar system that bring up strong emotions (positive or negative)?

   ♦ Did anything surprise you?

   ♦ Are there patterns that you would like to change? Maintain?

   ♦ Can you identify what actions to take to change or maintain them?

— CONNECTING OUR SOLAR SYSTEM TO BOUNDARY SETTING —

The following questions help connect the solar system exercise to different boundary-setting skills:

   ♦ How might the different boundary-setting skills, such as NAME THE BEHAVIOR, GIVE A DIRECTIVE, or the BROKEN RECORD, be used differently with different people on your solar system?

- Who in your solar system is also in your support system? Is there anyone who is not included that you would like to have in your support system?

- Who would be part of your REFLECTIVE LOOP? Why? What role would they play (critical and constructive feedback, emotional support, etc.)?

BOUNDARY-SETTING WRITING EXERCISES

These writing exercises can be done as journal entries where you answer the question specifically, or as a free write where you simply write what comes into your head in response to the questions for five minutes (you can do more if you like) without stopping or putting the pen down. They can be used as topics for group discussion topic or something to discuss in your relationships, friendships, or individually.

- How can boundaries help me create the kinds of relationships I want?

- How can boundaries help me nurture the relationships I have that I want to keep?

- How can the skills and tools discussed in this book be used to increase compassion for myself? For others?

- How can I use boundaries to enact my values? To work toward building the kind of community or communities that uphold varied yet shared values of liberation and justice?

- How can I use boundaries to create accountability?

— HOW DO WE DO WHAT WE DO? —

This exercise explores the myths of what it means to be a "good" activist and some of the expectations that may be placed on activists and those committed to social justice. You will be drawing an image of yourself and then filling it in as you go through the exercise. After you finish the drawing, you'll explore a series of questions to help you reflect.

Draw an outline of yourself on the left side of a sheet of blank paper. For now, leave the right side blank and leave a little bit of room at the top. After you draw yourself, write "What are some of the qualities that may be expected of a good/effective activist?" across the top. List them inside the outline of yourself. Some examples may include: humble, articulate, dedicated, loyal, hardworking, able or willing to work for low pay/no health care, generous with time or money, kind, caring, compassionate, willing to take risks, intelligent, and passionate. These are qualities we may or may not have, or may or may not want or value. They may be expectations we have for ourselves or for others, or expectations placed on us by other people or work cultures/structures.

Once you finish filling in the outline of your body with the qualities, you will begin to divide them into two categories as best you can. There will be some overlap and that's okay. This exercise is more about the process of exploring expectations and the impact they have than which quality gets placed into which category. Take two different color pens. Use one color to circle all the qualities that feed your soul, give you energy, contribute to your sense of self or your sense of vibrancy, help you feel connected to yourself, to other people and/or the work, or are in line with your values. With the other color, circle all the things that drain you; take up your time/energy in ways that do not feel good; contribute to a sense of disconnection from yourself, to others, and/or the work; deplete your sense of self or vibrancy; or may not fit in with your values. You can circle both or not circle some.

Now, take a moment to reflect. You can use the questions below to help generate self-reflection or dialogue if you are doing this exercise with a group:

- ◆ What came up for you emotionally, physically, or mentally as you did this exercise?

- ◆ What myths or ideas about the ideal activist are embodied by what you circled?

- Did you circle something with both colors? If so, how can you create balance here? Is balance necessary in this instance? Why or why not?

- Are there things that surprised you? Why?

- Which qualities are not written inside your body outline that you would like to include?

- Are there any qualities that you included but that you would now like to not have inside your outline? Why? Are there ways to use boundary setting to remove them?

MOVING FROM JUDGMENT TO NON-JUDGMENT EXERCISE

In this next exercise, you will fill in answers to two sets of questions in order to explore how judgment plays a role in your experiences, feelings, and behaviors. In the first set, you will be looking at how you respond to events, the internal dialogue that arises from events, and reflecting on how your internal dialogue affects your emotions and behaviors. In the second set, you will explore alternative and nonjudgmental ways of responding to events.

Start with an event then go through the corresponding list, filling in your emotional response, the judgment that arises, your emotional response to the judgment, and then identify the resulting behavior(s). The second list provides a way to practice using nonjudgmental language and frameworks for responding to events. There is an example to get you started. Note that the event and emotional response are the same in each list. This is because you are not trying to change your emotional response to an event or something that activates strong emotions or sensations. As you explore your responses and learn new skills, your emotions may change. But the goal is not to change your emotions; rather it is to be mindful of your thoughts and behaviors. In other words, we are not trying to control our emotions, but change our responses to them.

— JUDGMENT AND THE RESPONSE PATTERN —

Event/action: being late for work

Emotional response: guilt

Judgment: I am a bad person

Emotional response to judgment: shame

Resulting behavior: isolation; telling yourself you don't deserve to take a lunch break

---

— NON-JUDGMENT RESPONSE PATTERN —

Event/action: being late for work

Emotional response: guilt

Mindful response: identify feelings and sensations in the body (e.g., I feel guilty, I feel tingling in my jaw, a tightness in my belly, an urge to run, toes tensed, etc.)

Emotional response to mindfulness: acceptance of feeling guilty, using breath and hand on chest to ground and calm alongside guilty feeling

---

Resulting behavior: self-compassion (*everyone is late once in a while*), acceptance (*I feel guilty* and *I haven't done anything wrong*)

Resources and Resiliency

This next exercise explores various kinds of resources. There are many different types of resources, and their availability to us is informed by our experiences, the environment, our emotional, physical, mental, and spiritual capacities, trauma, economic factors, and social and relational considerations, to name a few. Some of the elements of this exercise are pulled from Sensorimotor Psychotherapy and the work of Pat Ogden.

For the purpose of this exercise, a "resource" is defined as a skill, ability, object, relationship, and/or service that provides support for maintaining a sense of self and differentiation from others, regardless of what is occurring in the environment. According to Pat Ogden, founder of the Sensorimotor Psychotherapy Institute, "When individuals are resourced, they are able to adjust and respond in a balanced and creative way to a wide variety of events and interactions, effectively sustaining autonomy in the face of stressful relational situations."

Read through the list below of various types of resources, and then read through the reflection questions to help you explore your current and desired relationship to the different resources. The list below is not exhaustive, but rather intended to provide a place to start thinking about different ways we can identify, access, tend to, develop, or choose to use resources.

— TYPES OF RESOURCES —

◆ Relational/interpersonal/social

Examples: friends, family, coworkers, members of groups you are apart of, mentors, peers, teachers, supervisors

◆ Somatic/physical

Examples: mindfulness, curiosity and ability to notice what is happening in your body, any kind of movement, breathing, various forms of exercise, feeling your body's response to pleasant and even neutral experiences (nice meal, cool breeze, bird sounds, etc.), moving meditation (could include very small movements of the body such as a slight lift of a finger or toe), martial arts, singing, dancing, touch, massage, body work

◆ Spiritual/faith-based/religious

Examples: church groups, fellowships, faith practices and rituals, spiritual beliefs and values, social networks grounded in faith or spiritual beliefs, choirs, nature oriented groups or activities

◆ Emotional/feeling

Examples: ability to identify and experience a range of different feelings, using emotions as an important source of information, wise mind (a balance or blend of both intellect and emotion)

◆ Intellectual/mental/cognitive

Examples: ability to reason, use logic, or intellectual skills to gather information or assess situations; problem-solving; observing facts; wise mind (a balance or blend of both intellect and emotion)

◆ Artistic/creative/appreciative of the arts

Examples: artwork; music; dance; theater; writing; performing; reading; enjoyment of all kinds of art; participating as an audience member, patron, or supporter; appreciation for the natural world and art in the environment; a sense of curiosity and wonder

◆ Nature/outdoors/physical world

Examples: playing in a park, hiking, lying in grass, staring at a flower, growing a garden, planting a seed, observing the seasons, watching clouds, staring out your window, going outside, being present to the out-of-doors, using the five senses to experience the world around you

- Material/environmental

  Examples: shelter, food, having basic material needs met, work or employment needs are met, health care, access to essential social and/or community supports

— CATEGORIES OF RESOURCES —

- Survival resources are resources that you use to cope or "get through" crisis situations.

  Examples: fight or flight, seeking medical help, heightened alertness

- Creative resources are resources that improve and develop your integrative capacity, improve your quality of life, your internal experiences, and promote a sense of competency and connectedness with self and others.

  Examples: doing an activity you enjoy, letting yourself play, attending social, artistic, religious, spiritual community or other kinds of important events, prioritizing enjoyable hobbies

- Existing resources are resources that are available and accessible in the present.

  Examples: breath, focus on a pleasing image or sound, boundary setting, ask for support, take a break, engage in self-care

- Missing resources are resources that were never developed, are incomplete, have been interrupted or are currently inaccessible for some reason.

  Examples: an inability to set some forms of boundaries, unable to ask for wanted/needed support, unsure how to identify desired self-care strategies

◆ Internal resources are resources that reside within you; the resources and the ability to use them are inside you.

Examples: experience pleasant sensations such as contentment, self-reflection, or contemplation, self-directed compassion or validation, sense of hope, faith, values, spiritual connections

◆ External resources refer to resources that reside outside of yourself.

Examples: social supports, financial resources, access to events, groups, activities, pets

— REFLECTION —

Thinking about the different types of resources above, take a few minutes to list of all the various kinds of resources you have currently. Then take a few minutes to envision the kinds of resources you want to develop. You can also reflect on any resources you used to have and would like to reconnect with. This should be done with nonjudgmental curiosity. Our resources change, expand, and contract for a variety of reasons. You can also use the chart below to look at how you habitually use resources and identify any changes you want to make.

ACTIVATING EVENT	HABITUAL REACTION
Resources used	Potential resources
	Resources you have used in the past
	Resources you can/want to use in the future
Three steps to take to integrate that resource	Identify any barriers to using the new resources and steps you can take to address the barriers.
	Identify any ways that boundary setting or using boundary-setting skills can help you develop resources.

Below is a list of additional questions to reflect on/write about:

1. What survival resources do you currently use?

2. What survival resources would you like to develop?

3. What are three steps you can take to develop some additional survival resources?

4. What creative resources do you currently have available?

5. Are there any creative resources you would like to develop? How might you do this?

6. What existing resources do you have?

7. What resources are missing?

8. Have they been interrupted? If so, how?

9. Are certain resources no longer accessible for some reason? How might you reintegrate them?

10. Which internal resources do you already have? Which would you like to develop?

11. Which external resources do you have? Which would you like to develop?

These are a few exercises to help you explore different aspects of what has been covered in this book. Play around with them, try out different things; if you have an idea of what might work better with a particular exercise, try it out. These are not written in stone, and all of them have, and will continue to be, changed as instructors, facilitators, and participants tinker with them. The most important thing is not to get a specific set of answers from a particular exercise or that you do it "right." The most important thing is that these exercises help you explore boundaries, self-care, and ways of envisioning the kinds of lives, relationships, systems, institutions, and communities you want to work toward.

ABOUT THE AUTHOR

CRISTIEN STORM IS A MENTAL HEALTH THERAPIST, cofounder and former director of Home Alive, where she developed and facilitated self-defense and boundary-setting curriculums rooted in social justice and progressive liberation theory. Currently, she is a cofounder of If You Don't They Will, a Seattle-based collaboration that provides concrete and creative strategies to counter white nationalism through a cultural lens. Storm also facilitates trainings and workshops on boundary setting, self-care, and resiliency theory and strategy.

For information or to schedule a reading or workshop:
cristien@cristienstorm.com
www.cristienstorm.com
empoweredboundaries.com.

About North Atlantic Books

North Atlantic Books (NAB) is an independent, nonprofit publisher committed to a bold exploration of the relationships between mind, body, spirit, and nature. Founded in 1974, NAB aims to nurture a holistic view of the arts, sciences, humanities, and healing. To make a donation or to learn more about our books, authors, events, and newsletter, please visit www.northatlanticbooks.com.

North Atlantic Books is the publishing arm of the Society for the Study of Native Arts and Sciences, a 501(c)(3) nonprofit educational organization that promotes cross-cultural perspectives linking scientific, social, and artistic fields. To learn how you can support us, please visit our website.